James Graham

Eden's Empire

T0262501

B L O O M S B U R Y
LONDON · NEW DELHI · NEW YORK · SYDNEY

Bloomsbury Methuen Drama

An imprint of Bloomsbury Publishing Plc

50 Bedford Square   1385 Broadway
London   New York
WC1B 3DP   NY 10018
UK   USA

www.bloomsbury.com

Bloomsbury is a registered trade mark of Bloomsbury Publishing Plc

First published in 2006 by Methuen Drama
Published by Methuen 2006

© James Graham 2006

Visit www.bloomsbury.com to find out more about our authors and their books
You will find extracts, author interviews, author events and you can sign up for
newsletters to be the first to hear about our latest releases and special offers.

British Library Cataloguing-in-Publication Data
A catalogue record for this book is available from the British Library.

ISBN: PB: 978-0-7136-8378-3
      EPDF: 978-1-4725-3703-4
      EPUB: 978-1-4725-3792-8

Library of Congress Cataloging-in-Publication Data
A catalog record for this book is available from the Library of Congress.

finboroughtheatre

[new **british** plays season 2006]

Pyre Productions and the **finborough**theatre
present

The World Premiere of

Eden's Empire

by James Graham

Eden's Empire was commissioned for the Finborough Theatre's
[new **british** plays season 2006] by Artistic Director Neil McPherson.

First performance at the Finborough Theatre.
Wednesday, 6 September 2006

The Pearson Playwrights' Scheme

The Pearson Playwrights' Scheme awards five bursaries a year to writers of outstanding promise. Each award allows the playwright a twelve-month attachment to a theatre and commissions the writers for a new play.

Previous recipients include Richard Bean, David Eldridge, Catherine Johnson, Charlotte Jones, Nick Leather, Martin McDonagh, Chloe Moss, Joe Penhall and Simon Stephens.

Applications are invited via theatres in October of each year and judged by a high profile panel, chaired by Sir John Mortimer QC CBE.

Previous winners for the Finborough Theatre include Chris Lee in 2000 for *On Line and Paranoid in the Sentimental City* and Laura Wade in 2005 for *Colder Than Here* which also won the Pearson Award for the Best Play written by a bursary winner. For the second year running, the Finborough Theatre is the only unfunded theatre to win a Pearson Bursary.

The Finborough Theatre has the support of the Pearson Playwrights' Scheme, supported by the Peggy Ramsay Foundation.

Eden's Empire

by James Graham

Cast in order of appearance
Anthony Eden
Winston Churchill **Ted Pleasance**
Reporter **Michael Kirk**
Byrnes **Nigel Pegram**
Molotov **Hayward Morse**
Caricaturist **Selva Rasalingam**
Lady Clarissa Eden **Daisy Beaumont**
Schuman **Nigel Pegram**
Colonel Nasser **Selva Rasalingam**
Dulles **Hayward Morse**
Harold Macmillan **Jamie Newall**
Butler **Hayward Morse**
Swinton **Michael Kirk**
Woolton **Nigel Pegram**
Frederick Bishop **Nigel Pegram**
Selwyn Lloyd **Michael Kirk**
Anthony Nutting **Selva Rasalingam**
Lord Mountbatten **Hayward Morse**
All other parts will be played by members of the Company.

The play is set between 1945 and 1957.

The performance lasts approximately two hours.

There will be one interval of fifteen minutes

Directed by **Gemma Fairlie**
Designed by **Alex Marker**
Lighting by **Matt Peel**
Sound by **Steve Mayo**
Costume Design by **Nell Knudsen**
Choreography by **Lynne Page**
Produced by **Marie Bobin**
Presented by Pyre Productions and the **finborough**theatre

Daisy Beaumont Clarissa Eden

Daisy trained with the National Youth Theatre and at the Webber Douglas Academy of Dramatic Art. Theatre includes Kevin Elyot's *The Day I Stood Still* (National Theatre), Alan Ayckbourn's *Virtual Reality* (Stephen Joseph Theatre, Scarborough), *Private Lives* and *The Ten Pound Look* (also Stephen Joseph Theatre, Scarborough) and *Two Tracks and Text Me* (West Yorkshire Playhouse). TV includes *This Life, The Stretch, In Deep, Poirot - The Murder of Roger Ackroyd, Close Relations* and *Down to Earth*. Film includes *Miracle at Midnight, The World Is Not Enough, Ten Minutes Older, I'll Sleep When I'm Dead* and *The Man Who Would Be Queen*. Radio includes *Bleak House, Hotel Europa, Murder on the Leviathan* and *King Trash*. Daisy is also a founder member of Bacchae Productions and is currently both writing and producing for them.

Michael Kirk Selwyn Lloyd / Swinton / Reporter

Theatre includes *The Great Highway* (The Gate), *Born in Gilead* (Young Vic), *Jack and the Beanstalk* (Hackney Empire), *Amadeus* and *Macbeth* (Derby Playhouse), *My Fair Lady* (Theatre Royal Drury Lane), *Farm* (Greenwich Theatre), *Love's a Luxury, Abigail's Party* and *Roughyheads* (Oldham Coliseum), *Great Expectations* (Walnut Street Theatre, Philadelphia), *How The Other Half Loves* and *Martin Chuzzlewit* (Nottingham Playhouse), *The Crucible, To Serve Them All My Days* and *Breezeblock Park* (Royal Theatre, Northampton), *Pal Joey* and *Romeo and Juliet* (Bristol Old Vic), *The Pickwick Papers* and *Measure for Measure* (Everyman Theatre, Cheltenham), *Winner Takes All* and *Rabenthal* (Wolsey Theatre, Ipswich), *Victoriana* (New End, Hampstead) and National Tours of *Present Laughter, Candida, Pygmalion, Murder by Misadventure, Twelfth Night* and *Ghosts*. West End Theatre includes *Me and My Girl, Oliver!, The Rocky Horror Show, Foul Play* and *As You Like it*. Film and TV includes *The Voice, SongBird, Lullabelle, Casualty, London's Burning, North Square, Victoria and Albert, Crack, EastEnders, High Jynx, The Mummy's Tomb* and *The Chief*.

Hayward Morse

Lord Mountbatten / Molotov / Dulles / Butler

Hayward Morse trained at RADA and then worked with regional theatres until making his London debut in the original production of Joe Orton's *What The Butler Saw*. He remained in the West End for the musical *Canterbury Tales* and the first stage version of *The Rocky Horror Picture Show* and travelling to New York received a Tony Award nomination for his performance in the Broadway production of Simon Gray's *Butley*. Since then, he has appeared in many film, television, radio and stage productions internationally encompassing the West End, Canada's Shaw and Shakespeare Festivals and English theatres in Europe. Recent work includes *Travels With My Aunt* (Birmingham Repertory Theatre) and an episode of *Footballer's Wives* (ITV). He has recorded over one hundred Audio Books of all types.

Jamie Newall Harold Macmillan
Jamie was born in Edinburgh and trained at Bristol Old Vic Theatre School. Theatre includes Judd in *Another Country* (Queen's Theatre), *Richard III* , *Henry V, Love's Labour's Lost, Hamlet, Red Noses, A Christmas Carol* (Royal Shakespeare Companyy), a *Time Out* Award for Nathan Leopold in *Never The Sinner* (Offstage), *The Great Pretenders,* Robespierre in *Danton's Death* (Gate), Abel Drugger in *The Alchemist* (National Theatre), The Actor in *The Woman In Black* (Fortune Theatre), Osric and the Player Queen in *Hamlet* (Elsinore), Don Pedro in *Much Ado About Nothing* (AFTLS US Tour), Castel in The Tunnel of Obsession* (Croydon Warehouse and
Edinburgh Festival) and *Stephen in Crossings* (Sgript Cymru at Cardiff, Arcola Theatre, London and Traverse Theatre, Edinburgh). Jamie has also appeared in repertory in Harrogate, Coventry, Salisbury, Edinburgh, Sheffield, Nottingham, Birmingham, Watford, Stoke, Manchester in such roles as Leontes in *The Winter's Tale,* Simon in *Hay Fever,* Antonio in *The Duchess Of Malfi,* Davoren in *The Shadow Of A Gunman,* Simon in *Mary Rose,* Willie Mossop in *Hobson's Choice,* Trofimov in *The Cherry Orchard,* Nero in *Britannicus,* the title role in *Dr. Faustus,* Corvino in *Volpone,* Languebeau Snuffe in *The Atheist's Tragedy,* John and Tod in *Nothing Compares To You,* All the D'Ascoynes in *Kind Hearts and Coronets,* Roy in *Neville's Island,* Aguecheek in *Twelfth Night,* Chasuble and Algernon in *The Importance Of Being Earnest,* Winston Splinter in *Krindlekrax,* Julius Winterhalter in *Waters Of the Moon,* Gerald in *Woman In Mind* and Philip Lester in *A Touch of the Sun.* TV includes *A Class of His Own, Trelawny of the Wells, Yes Prime Minister, Devices and Desires, Sex Guys and Videotape, Casualty* and *The Bill.* Radio includes *Friends Of Oscar, Baltasar and Blimunda, The Mouse that Roared, Colonel Warburton's Madness, McClevy* and *Flash For Freedom!.*

Nigel Pegram
 Sir Frederick Bishop / Byrnes/ Schuman / Woolton
Nigel appeared in the 1964 Oxford Revue at the Edinburgh Festival with Michael Palin and Terry Jones, and then spent six months with The Second City Company in Chicago in 1965, Nigel joined the cast of *Wait A Minim,* starring both in the West End and on Broadway for its 15 month run. During his time in New York, he studied at The Actors Studio with Lee Strasberg. His many theatre roles include the Duke of Windsor in the UK tour of *Crown Matrimonial,* "The Watchdog Man" Melvyn P. Thorpe in *The Best Little Whorehouse in Texas* (Theatre Royal Drury Lane), Wilson in *The Case of the Dead Flamingo,* Tullus, King
of Rome in *Horace* (Lyric Studio, Hammersmith) and most recently Old Adam and Sir Oliver Martext in Sir Peter Hall's UK and US tour of *As You Like It.* His many TV appearances include *Robert's Robots, The Tomorrow People, Get Some In, The Professionals, The Singing Detective, Drop the Dead Donkey, Lovejoy, Van Der Valk, Doctors,* Inspector Wexford in *Road Rage* and three series of *Outside Edge* in which he

played Nigel, a part specially written for him. Films include *Proteus*, *Princess Daisy*, *Diana – Her True Story* and *The American Way* with Denis Hopper and Michael J. Pollard in which he played Willa Westinghouse, the first female candidate for the President of the United States. He is married to ex Royal Ballet soloist and actress, April Olrich.

Ted Pleasance Winston Churchill

Trained at The Actor's Centre. He started his career as a Radio Officer in the Merchant Navy and was stationed aboard a luxury yacht based in Monte Carlo when Sir Winston was a frequent guest of Aristotle Onassis aboard his yacht *Christina*. He left to take up a scholarship to read Philosophy, Politics and Economics at Oxford. After postgraduate study, he worked in Central Government on Industrial Relations and Employment issues. He took up acting after leaving the public service. Theatre includes Uncle George in Brian Friel's *Aristocrats* at the (National Theatre), Lord Nobby Clarke in *This Is Your Captain Speaking* (Pentameters Theatre, Hampstead), Ivan Zhukov in *Russian National Mail* (Barbican), Dr Ivan Ivic in *Cargo* (Oval House) and *The Crucible* (Birmingham Rep. Company tour). TV includes Tony Martin in *The Tony Martin Story* (BBC), *Kenya: White Terror* and *Unit 371* (both for BBC). Film includes *Strange Neighbours*, *Boxes*, *Why?*, *The Gaffer* and *Pistachio*. Ted was a member of the church choir when Winston Churchill was installed as the Lord Warden of the Cinque Ports at Dover Castle in 1948.

Selva Rasalingam

Colonel Nasser / Anthony Nutting/ Caricaturist

Trained at the Guildhall School of Music and Drama. Theatre includes Leicester in *Mary Stuart* (Derby Playhouse), Moazzam Begg in *Guantanamo - Honor Bound to Defend Freedom* (Tricycle Theatre and New Ambassadors), Shiva in *Midnight's Children* (Royal Shakespeare Company UK and US tour), Vincent in *The Woman Who Swallowed a Pin* (The Lab at Southwark Playhouse), Polixenes in *The Winter's Tale* (Southwark Playhouse), Sir Lancelot in *Merlin* (Riverside Studios), Albert Adam in *The Play's the Thing* (Merlin International Theatre, Budapest). TV includes *Britain's First Suicide Bombers* (BBC), *Lost in Egypt: Decoding the Papyri* (BBC), Herod in *Secrets of Herod's Reign* (National Geographic / La7 / Fremantle), *The Bill* (ITV), *Joseph - The Bible Story* (BBC, SkyOne, Turner Network Television), *Jonathan Creek* (BBC), *Real Men* (BBC), *Holby City* (BBC), *Murder in Mind* (BBC), *Dream Team* (Sky One), *Bad Girls* (ITV) and Arthur Miller's *The Golden Years* (Channel 4). Film includes *Man About Dog*, *Anita and Me*, *Son of the Pink Panther* and *Carry On Columbus*.

James Graham Playwright

James Graham is currently Pearson Playwright-in-Residence at the Finborough Theatre where his play *Albert's Boy* was premiered in 2005 to commemorate Einstein Year and the 60th anniversary of the atomic bombing of Hiroshima and Nagasaki. The play earned James a prestigious Pearson Playwriting Bursary. His first play, *Coal not Dole!*, played at the Edinburgh Festival in 2002 and subsequently toured the North of England. James is also a member of the Royal Court Young Writers' Programme and was the Finborough Theatre's representative as one of the BBC and Royal Court's '50' emerging writers as part of the Royal Court's 50th anniversary celebrations. James is currently under commission to develop a comedy drama with TV producers Greenlit.

Gemma Fairlie Director

Gemma trained at Edinburgh University and Mountview Academy. She won the Gate Theatre's directing bursary in 2004 and earlier this year completed the National Theatre's Directors Course. Past Directing includes *Silence* by Moira Buffini (The Other Place, Stratford-upon-Avon, and Arcola Theatre), *For Every Passion Something* (RSC Learning Residency in USA), *St. Erkenwald* (Oxford School of Drama), *Protect Me From What I Want* (Young Vic Studio), *The Memory of Water* (Barons Court), *The Frog Prince* and *Same Old Story* (Cockpit Theatre). Previous Assisting includes the RSC's Regional Tour of *Julius Caesar* and *The Two Gentlemen of Verona*, a national tour of *Carousel* (UK Productions) and *Happy Yet?* (Gate). She has just assisted and choreographed the movement on Anthony Neilson's *Realism* (National Theatre of Scotland and Edinburgh International Festival). In October, she will direct for RSC Learning in Detroit as part of their Michigan Residency.

Alex Marker Designer

Trained in Theatre Design at Wimbledon School of Art and has designed over forty productions. He is Associate Designer of the Finborough Theatre where his recent credits include *The Representative, Red Night, Lark Rise to Candleford, Albert's Boy, Hortensia and the Museum of Dreams, Trelawny of the 'Wells', Soldiers Happy Family, How I Got That Stor* and *The Women's War - a Centenary Celebration.* Future designs include the premiere of Keith Dewhurst's new play *King Arthur* (Arcola Theatre). Other Designs include *Oklahoma!* (New Wimbledon Theatre), *Marat/Sade* (Northampton), *Cooking With Elvis, Gym and Tonic, The Opposite Sex* and *Inside Job* (Lyceum Theatre, Crewe), *Hush* (Pleasance, Edinburgh and Arcola Theatre), *Twelfth Night* and *Been So Long* (Broadway Theatre, Catford), *Marília Pêra Sings Ary Barroso* (Bloomsbury Theatre), *Oedipus, Agamemnon* and *Androcles and the Lion* (The Scoop), *A Doll's House, The Ruffian on the Stair* and *The Erpingham Camp* (Greenwich Playhouse). He also recently designed an exhibition to commemorate the 100th anniversary of Brentford Football club held at Gunnersbury Park Museum in London. Alex's Great Great Grandfather George Marker was one of the first people to sail down the Suez Canal as part of the crew of HMS *Royal Oak* at the official opening in November 1869. www.nukinetics.com/alexmarker

Matt Peel Lighting

Lighting includes *Silence* (RSC Fringe and London), *Paradox* (RSC Fringe) and *Dr Foster* (RSC Fringe and London). Relights include *The Canterbury Tales* (RSC at the National Theatre of Barcelona and Almagro Festival). He was also Assistant Lighting Designer on *The Lion King* (Scheveningen, Netherlands).

Steve Mayo Sound

Steve has recently designed *Mythomania* (White Bear Theatre and Rosemary Branch), *A Tale of Two Cities* and *Cinderella* (Guildhall School of Music and Drama), *Silence* (RSC Fringe and Arcola Theatre), *Dr Foster* (RSC Fringe and Menier Chocolate Factory) and *Paradox* (RSC Fringe) as well as work at the Haymarket Theatre, Basingstoke, and Library Theatre, Manchester. Steve has spent the last year teaching sound at the Guildhall School of Music and Drama and is currently Sound Engineer on *Rock 'n' Roll* in the West End.

Nell Knudsen Costume Design

Trained in Fine Art at the Art College of Bergen, and in Costume for the Screen and Stage at the Arts Institute of Bournemouth. She is Associate Costume Designer of the Finborough Theatre where she designed costumes for *I Wish to Die Singing, Freedom of the City, Florodora, Blackwater Angel, Loyalties* and *Our Miss Gibbs* and was Costume Design Assistant for *Lark Rise to Candleford*. Other Theatres include *Immortal* (Courtyard Theatre, Covent Garden), *Anatol* (Arcola), *Guadeasmus or a Very Liberal Education* (Arcola) and *A Devilish Exercise, Conjuring Marlowe at the Rose* (The Rose Theatre, London). She was Costume Design Assistant for *The 5 Man Show* (The Linbury Studio, Royal Opera House and Tour). Films include six short films, including *Monicha Guildheart and the Mysterious Pencil*, (which won the Royal Television Award for Short Film 2004), and Costume Design Assistant for the feature film *Bigga Than Ben*. TV includes Costume Design for the TV-pilot *House Group*.

Marie Bobin Producer

Graduated from Emerson College, Boston, with a BA in Dramaturgy and Design. At the Finborough Theatre, she produced Tom Murphy's *The Gigli Concert* and James Graham's *Albert's Boy*. She has also produced and directed *A Thing of Beauty* (Los Angeles), *Sacha Guitry's French Season* (French Cultural Centre, Boston) and worked on Odyssey Theatre's productions of *The Good Woman of Setzuan* and *Brecht on Brecht* (Los Angeles). Marie is the Development Producer for the Finborough Theatre.

Neil McPherson Producer

Neil has been Artistic Director of the Finborough Theatre since January 1999. www.concordance.org.uk

Pyre Productions

Founded by Artistic Director Gemma Fairlie, Pyre Production's challenge is to make political theatre accessible to all and reveal the personal issues at the heart of each piece. We run workshops for all ages and abilities. We have taught in schools, colleges and Art Centres and have worked with amateur dramatic groups, professional artists and artists in training in Britain and internationally.

New British Plays at the Finborough Theatre

New British Plays at the Finborough Theatre over the last few years include the world premieres of Sarah Phelps' *Modern Dance for Beginners* (subsequently produced at the Soho Theatre), Carolyn Scott-Jeffs' sell-out comedy *Out in the Garden* (which transferred to the Assembly Rooms, Edinburgh) and *Tarnished Angel* (broadcast on Radio 4); *The Alchemist* – an adaptation of Paulo Coelho's novel; two plays specially commissioned for the Finborough – the London debut of Finborough Theatre Pearson Playwright-in-Residence Laura Wade with her adaptation of W.H. Davies' *Young Emma*, and Steve Hennessy's *Lullabies of Broadmoor* on the Finborough Road murder of 1922; Dameon Garnett's *Break Away*; the New British Plays Season 2005 featuring Simon Vinnicombe's *Year 10* which went on to play at BAC's *Time Out* Critics' Choice Season and at the International Theatre Festival, Strasbourg, James Graham's *Albert's Boy* with Victor Spinetti, winner of the prestigious Pearson Award; and Joy Wilkinson's *Fair* which transferred to the West End; as well as the London premieres of Sonja Linden's *I Have Before Me a Remarkable Document Given to Me by a Young Lady from Rwanda* (*Time Out* Critics' Choice and subsequently heard on Radio 4 and seen on National Tour) and Peter Oswald's *Lucifer Saved* with Mark Rylance. Many of the Finborough's new plays have been published.

finboroughtheatre

Artistic Director **Neil McPherson**
Associate Designer **Alex Marker**
Pearson Playwright-in-Residence **James Graham**
Playwrights-in-Residence –
   David Carter, Al Smith, Laura Wade and **Samantha Wright**
Literary Manager **Alexandra Wood**
Development Producer **Marie Bobin**
Associate Producer **Susannah Stevens**

Founded in 1980, the multi-award-winning Finborough Theatre presents new writing from the UK and overseas, music theatre and unjustly neglected work from the last 150 years.

In its first decade, artists working at the theatre included Rory Bremner, Clive Barker, Kathy Burke, Nica Burns, Ken Campbell and Clare Dowie (the world premiere of *Adult Child/Dead Child*). From 1991-1994, the theatre was at the forefront of the explosion of new writing with Naomi Wallace's first play *The War Boys*; Rachel Weisz in David Farr's *Neville Southall's Washbag* which later became the award-winning West End play, *Elton John's Glasses*; and three plays by Anthony Neilson - *The Year of the Family; Normal: the Dusseldorf Ripper*; and *Penetrator* which transferred from the Traverse and went on to play at the Royal Court Upstairs. From 1994, the theatre was run by The Steam Industry. Highlights included new plays by Tony Marchant, David Eldridge, Mark Ravenhill and Phil Willmott, new writing development including Mark Ravenhill's *Shopping and F***king* (Royal Court, West End and Broadway) and Naomi Wallace's *Slaughter City* (Royal Shakespeare Company), the UK premiere of David Mamet's *The Woods*, and Anthony Neilson's *The Censor* which transferred to the Royal Court.

Neil McPherson became Artistic Director in 1999. Notable productions since then have included the world premieres of Sarah Phelps' *Modern Dance for Beginners* (subsequently produced at the Soho Theatre), Carolyn Scott-Jeffs' sell-out comedy *Out in the Garden* (which transferred to the Assembly Rooms, Edinburgh); two plays specially commissioned for the Finborough - Laura Wade's adaptation of W.H. Davies' *Young Emma*, and Steve Hennessy's *Lullabies of Broadmoor* on the Finborough Road murder of 1922; the 2005 New British Plays Season featuring Simon Vinnicombe's *Year 10* (which went on to play at BAC's *Time Out* Critics' Choice Season and at the International Theatre Festival, Strasbourg), James Graham's *Albert's Boy* with Victor Spinetti, and Joy Wilkinson's *Fair* which transferred to the West End; as well as the London premieres of Sonja Linden's *I Have Before Me a Remarkable Document Given to Me by a Young Lady from Rwanda* and Peter Oswald's *Lucifer Saved* with Mark Rylance. UK premieres of foreign plays have included Brad Fraser's *Wolfboy*, Lanford Wilson's *Sympathetic Magic*, Larry Kramer's *The Destiny of Me*, Tennessee Williams' *Something Cloudy, Something Clear*, Frank McGuinness' *Gates of Gold* with William Gaunt and the late John Bennett in his last stage role, *Hortensia and the Museum of Dreams* with Linda Bassett and *Blackwater Angel*, the UK debut of Irish playwright Jim Nolan with Sean Campion. The Finborough's revivals of neglected work include the first London revivals of Rolf Hochhuth's *Soldiers*, both parts of Keith Dewhurst's *Lark Rise to Candleford* - performed in promenade and in repertoire, *The Gigli Concert* with Niall Buggy, Catherine Cusack and Paul McGann (which also transferred to the Assembly Rooms, Edinburgh), *The Women's War* – an evening of original suffragette plays, the Victorian comedy *Masks and Faces*, *Etta Jenks* with Clarke Peters and

Daniela Nardini, *Loyalties* by John Galsworthy, and an acclaimed series of musical theatre - *The Finborough Gaieties – Celebrating British Musical Theatre 1870-1914* with *Florodora* and *Our Miss Gibbs*.

The Finborough Theatre won the Guinness Award for Theatrical Ingenuity in 1996 and 1997; the Pearson Award bursary for writers Chris Lee in 2000, Laura Wade (also for Pearson Award Best Play) in 2005 and for James Graham in 2006; was shortlisted for the Empty Space Peter Brook Award in 2003 and 2004; and won the Empty Space Peter Brook Mark Marvin Award in 2004, and the Empty Space Peter Brook Award's prestigious Dan Crawford Pub Theatre Award in 2005.

You can read a full history of the theatre – and of the local area – at **www.finboroughtheatre.co.uk**

friends of the **finborough**theatre
The Finborough Theatre receives no public or private funding from any source, and relies solely on the support of our audiences. Please do consider supporting us by becoming a member of our newly relaunched Friends Scheme. There are four categories of Friends, each offering a wide range of benefits.
Brandon Thomas Friends – Anonymous. Nancy Balaban. Philip Hooker. Barbara Marker. Harry MacAuslan, Anthony Melnikoff. Barbara Naughton. Sylvia Young. Lionel Monckton Friends – Anonymous. Leopold Liebster

For *Eden's Empire*

Deputy Stage Manager	Edward Salt
Stage Manager	Sarah Brimble
Technical Operator	Emma Blundell
Scenic Painting	Scarlett Raven
Press Representative	press@finboroughtheatre.co.uk (020 7244 7439)
Production Photography	Marilyn Kingwill
Graphic Design	Matt @ Illustration Source

Pyre Productions and the Finborough Theatre would like to thank
Milo Twomey, Laurence Mitchell, Merryn Owen, Fenella Hunt, Philip Edgerley, Johnny Kemp, Mark Benson, Richard Walker, the Spiro Institute, the National Theatre of Scotland and the company of *Realism*, Royal Marines Association, Penny Black, Lyell and Maggie Fairlie, Briony Redman, Patrick Maplin, Kate O'Sullivan and Cactus Designs.

The Finborough Theatre is licensed by the Royal Borough of Kensington and Chelsea to The Steam Industry. The Steam Industry is under the Artistic Direction of Phil Willmott. www.philwillmott.co.uk The Steam Industry is a company limited by guarantee. Registered in England no. 3448268. Registered Charity no. 1071304. Registered Office: 118 Finborough Road, London SW10 9ED.

I would like to thank Gemma Fairlie and Neil McPherson for their help in developing the script; the Pearson Foundation, Sally Whitehill and Curtis Brown Ltd, Marie Bobin, Simon Stephens, The Royal Court, BBC Writersroom, Peter Kavanagh, Guy Chapman Associates Ltd and Methuen for their continued support; Roy and Sarah-Jane Dickenson; Ashfield School and The University of Hull Department of Drama; Ailsa, Jenny and Clare for their friendship; Jackie Sanders and David Brindley for theirs and more; my family, Mum and Dad especially, for their unparalleled care and commitment, then and now.

Most of all, credit deserves to go to Neil McPherson of the Finborough Theatre, for taking the risk with me on my first, and handing this to me, my second ...

- James Graham, August 2006

Eden's Empire

Characters

Anthony Eden, *Prime Minister (1955–57), fifties*
Lady Clarissa Eden, *his wife, thirties*
Harold Macmillan, *Chancellor of the Exchequer (1955–57),*
    fifties
Winston Churchill, *Prime Minister (1940–45 and 1951–55),*
    seventies
Colonel Nasser, *President of Egypt (1954–70), thirties*

An ensemble cast of four can share the following roles, or alternatively
one actor can take each part.

Selwyn Lloyd, *British Foreign Secretary (1955–62)*
Frederick Bishop, *Eden's Principal Private Secretary (1956–57)*
Anthony Nutting, *Minister of State, Foreign Office (1954–56)*
Earl Mountbatten, *First Sea Lord (1955–59)*
Molotov, *Russian Foreign Minister (1939–49 and 1953–56)*
Byrnes, *American Secretary of State (1945–47)*
Dulles, *American Secretary of State (1953–59)*
Schuman, *French Minister of Foreign Affairs (1948–53)*
Woolton, *Cabinet Minister*
Butler, *Cabinet Minister*
Viscount Swinton, *Cabinet Minister*
Dr Hume
Reporter
Caricaturist

A chorus of **Ministers**
Assembled **Figures** *(Potsdam)*

Act One

The Führerbunker, Hitler's former war rooms beneath the Reich Chancellery in Berlin, 1945. Complete darkness. There are shouts in Russian, off.

Eden (*off*)   Yes, yes thank you. We know. Through here.

A torchlight flashes around the stage. We catch glimpses of a desk, a map of the world on the wall, files. Footsteps in the room.

Right, according to . . . Yes, these were . . . well, his private quarters, I suppose. (*More flashes round of the torch.*) Oh. Mind, mind your step, Prime . . . Here, let me . . . find a –

The torchlight catches a red and white flag emblazoned with a Nazi swastika, and there is a pause where only this is seen. We hear a click, and overhead lighting in the room flickers on to reveal **Anthony Eden**, *standing by a light switch and holding a torch, and* **Winston Churchill**, *who stands, back turned to us, smoking a cigar, motionless, and taking in his surroundings of the cold concrete bunker.*

Eden (*looking around, barely audible*)   Winston . . .

A long silence. **Churchill** *shuffles around. He looks at the floor, at the map on the wall.* **Eden** *also takes an apprehensive glance around, anxious, expecting to discover something unpleasant.* **Churchill** *picks up a Bible from the desk, and shows it to* **Eden**, *who nods.* **Churchill** *replaces it, and stands for a moment in thought.*

Churchill   My chair was comfier than his.

Eden   Ours was warmer, too.

Churchill (*pause, then gesturing around, half-laughing, tragically*) Anthony. Did you ever imagine? (*Beat.*) Berlin looks worse than I feared. I am surprised they have welcomed us with such warmth.

Eden   We have set them free.

Churchill   No. No, they must do that for themselves.

Churchill *faces the map on the wall. He brushes his fingers across Britain. Pause.*

Churchill   Still! On to Potsdam, what?! To begin rebuilding.

Eden   Hear, hear.

Churchill   We must stay close to the Americans now that Truman is in charge. Roosevelt and Stalin were all over each other at Yalta like young lovers.

Eden   I'm keen to push for quick justice against those Nazis being held. We're working with the Americans on devising a trial. It's a little tricky, of course. Nothing like this has ever . . . Our chaps are playing with a charge of . . . 'crimes against humanity'.

Churchill   'Crimes against humanity'? What a thing to be guilty of.

He brushes his hand across the chair again.

Eden   Uh, through there, I believe . . . like yourself, he had a bedroom and . . . that's where he . . . though they warned of some blood still evident, so you might not want to −

Churchill *exits in the direction indicated by* **Eden**. *Pause.*
Churchill *returns, nods and exits.* **Eden** *flicks off the light and the bunker descends into darkness once more.*

The **Reporter** *appears, reading from his notepad, making alterations as he reads.*

Reporter   The much heralded . . . (*Scribbles.*) No, the much lauded . . . (*Scribbles.*) The great! − that's it − the great tripartite conference between allies Britain, Russia and America begins in Potsdam, near Berlin, today, following the German surrender. The 'bulldog', the 'bear' and, uh . . . (*Scribbles out.*) Misters Churchill, Stalin and Truman, in attendance with their foreign secretaries Mr Eden, Mr Byrnes and Mr Molotov . . .

Potsdam. A map of the world lit up on the floor. The room is dimly lit.

The tango theme creeps in as **Eden, Byrnes** *and* **Molotov** *enter. They embrace each other individually in dance holds and stride, stomp and turn into their seats, positioned as a semicircle in a pool of light, as chairs and other* **Figures** *assemble behind them.*

In the surrounding darkness are the shapes of other seated **Figures**, *with smoke billowing from cigarettes and cigars. Behind* **Eden**, *perhaps only his legs visible in the light, is* **Churchill**. *His hand extends frequently into the light, holding a note, and tapping* **Eden** *on the shoulder. Without a break in the dialogue,* **Eden** *always takes the note from over his shoulder, reads it, and then passes it back into the darkness. This happens frequently throughout. The equivalent happens between* **Byrnes** *and* **Molotov** *with the figures behind them.* **Eden, Byrnes** *and* **Molotov** *have notes on their laps that they refer to. Amongst the other* **Figures** *seated, barely visible in the dark, perpetual note-passing occurs and continues ritualistically throughout.*

Eden   So we are agreed on the draft ultimatum for Japan?

Byrnes   Of course agreed. Our boys are still engaged there and we need a resolution fast.

Molotov   We would also suggest the United States do not keep this new weapon of theirs under their hat. Rather they use it as a bargaining point.

Eden   Very well. Japan must surrender to the Allied forces immediately. (*Copying from a sheet.*) 'The alternative . . . is prompt . . . and utter . . . destruction.' (*Pause.*) Right.

They tick something off on a sheet. A common occurrence, even when not mentioned.

Establishing a Council of Foreign Ministers to deliver peace treaties to those who've surrendered and answer outstanding territorial questions. We three shall act as chief representatives, but to ensure a lasting peace, Britain wishes to submit France as well.

Byrnes   Agreed.

Molotov   Agreed, if China may join also.

Byrnes   I'm afraid my government simply cannot acknowledge China as a power, Mr Molotov. It would make this Council's policies unenforceable.

Molotov   They will be unenforceable if the world's fifth great power is missing.

Eden   Perhaps additions can be negotiated later. Can we at least agree to London being the permanent seat of the joint secretariat?

Molotov   Can it move to other capitals from time to time? Just as a change?

Byrnes   Yeah. That would be nice.

Eden (*beat*)   Agreed. Next.

Byrnes   Regarding the peace treaties, we would like Italy to be the first of the fallen Axis Powers to receive theirs, as they were first to sever ties with Hitler.

Eden   We won't have a problem with that.

Molotov *shrugs.*

Eden   On to Germany. The Yalta agreement dictates each occupying force shall govern the zones their troops currently occupy. (*Opens a map.*) To clarify, Russia shall be in charge from here in the east, Britain here, America here and there, and we'll give France that.

Byrnes   The Soviets have submitted their application to extend their authority across the whole of Austria. Mr Eden, my recommendation is we allow this once our troops are stationed there. Perhaps Vienna?

Molotov   Why? Our troops are already stationed there. (*Receives note from behind.*) Fine.

Byrnes   Poland, and what territories should return to the provisional government.

Eden (*opens the map*)   The new proposal would see the Soviet-occupied territories east of this line, running from the Baltic, west of Swinemuende, along the Oder to the Czech frontier, returning to Poland and not withheld by the Soviets.

Molotov   Wait. This has barely changed from the first draft, if at all.

Byrnes   This isn't a war anyone can gain from, Mr Molotov. The land belonged to Poland.

Molotov   So after my countrymen died to save this land, are dying in occupation, we are to walk out and leave us with no barrier of defences? We cannot accept this proposal until representatives visit the area.

Byrnes   We should wait until the peace treaty has been signed anyway.

Molotov   No, no more delays. If no good alternative is produced, we shall not withdraw.

Eden (*receiving a note over his shoulder. Pause*)   What if we gave you Czechoslovakia?

Molotov (*pause*)   Czechoslovakia is no good to us. It cannot protect us.

Byrnes   Maybe we could negotiate over Danzig.

Eden   No. That would mean the new Poland is completely landlocked.

Molotov (*with the map*)   Well . . . (*Sighs.*) What about Koenigsberg?

Byrnes (*beat*)   We'd be willing to negotiate Koenigsberg.

Molotov   With the transfer of all existing residents back to Poland?

Byrnes (*beat*)   Agreed.

Eden (*beat*)   Agreed.

Byrnes   As for the future, it is the job of the Allied Control Council and the responsibility of the German people to redirect their lives to a peaceful democratic basis and retake their place amongst the free people of the world.

Molotov (*with his notes*)   Guidelines include the full disarmament of Germany and the annihilation of the National Socialist Party. The Allied Council also assumes the authority to reverse every law passed by the Party.

Eden   Additionally, the destruction of all arms and decommissioning of the armed forces.

Molotov (*laughing*)   I think you'll find my forces have already done that for you, Mr Eden.

Byrnes   Should we maybe consider delegating some of the arms between us?

Molotov   It does seem a waste.

Eden   Perhaps. Let us maybe establish what has survived first? With regard to the economy, an emphasis on shifting it from arms production, metals and chemicals, to things such as . . . (*Writing.*) agriculture, farming and . . . (*Thinks.*) fishing?

Molotov (*pause, then shrugs*)   Mm-hmm. Fishing.

Byrnes (*overlaps, mumbling*)   Yeah, fishing sounds fine.

Eden   Very well. The war crimes trial for those captured prisoners.

Byrnes   Right. Now, the arrests are still continuing. Needless to say, we still have some pretty big catches in our net. Including Speer and Goering, of course.

Eden   And we are as adamant as the Americans that a fair and just trial be given to them.

Molotov   You won't seriously let them defend themselves. We should just execute them.

Eden   They must be tried under the international law of the new United Nations body. We must not resort to the injustices they did. This is a message to the world. We are now all accountable for every wrong we commit on this planet. Inside or outside of war. Only then can we hope neither our predecessors nor we ever again find ourselves sitting where we are today. The object is peace, gentlemen. Let us continue.

Potsdam begins to fade into darkness amidst a frenzied exchange of handshakes between parties. The **Reporter** *appears, independent of this action, holding a newspaper. Next to him, the* **Caricaturist**, *who scribbles frantically on a pad of paper.*

Reporter   Results are in, Fred. State of the parties: Conservatives 180, Labour 364! It's a veritable landslide!

Caricaturist   Blimey. Well . . . that's it, then. He's out.

Reporter   So it'll be Attlee and Bevin wrapping up Potsdam then. Word is, the old boy's taking it personally, Fred.

Caricaturist   Well you would, Bill, wouldn't you? I mean, you just would.

Reporter   Yeah. Shame. In a way.

Caricaturist   'Tis a shame.

Reporter   Some might even say ungrateful.

Caricaturist   Yeah. They might.

Churchill's *quarters.* **Eden** *and* **Churchill** *flick on a couple of dim desk lamps.*

Churchill (*solemnly*)   Was it really as bad as all that?

Eden   I'm afraid it rather was, yes. Even Wimbledon went Labour.

Churchill   Heavens. The game is really up. (*Pause.*) Though I suppose this is the democracy we have been fighting and dying for. And it has been exercised with vigour. I cannot judge them poorly, Anthony. For poorly is what they are. We have bestowed upon them nothing bar hardship and pain.

Eden   This doesn't mean they do not love you, Winston. All they want is change.

Churchill   The next few years protesting from the shadows. Perhaps this is an ideal time for you to take over, Anthony. And me to step down. It feels like the end.

Eden   Or a new beginning. Perhaps.

Churchill (*smiles*)   My Anthony. What will you do? I hate to think of you all alone now.

Eden   Well, there's still my Warwick and Leamington seat, of course.

Churchill   Well, you are always welcome with me. (*Beat.*) I know my niece, Clarissa, is . . . very fond of your visits . . .

He disappears as **Clarissa** *appears.* **Eden** *bows. Waltz music swells. They embrace in a dance hold and begin to turn, slowly.*

Clarissa   I remember when you first came round. All those years ago.

Eden   You were ever so shy.

Clarissa   I was sixteen! And you were this . . . *man.* (*Laughs.*) Your tweed jacket and pinstriped trousers!

Eden   What's wrong with my tweed jacket and pinstriped trousers?

Clarissa   No, nothing. Very English and . . . what's the − debonair.

Eden   Yes, I forget I'm conversing with a professional fashion expert. Must watch what I wear more carefully from now on.

Clarissa   Well, these things are important. Especially in politics.

Eden   They didn't used to be.

Clarissa (*pause*)   I was . . . ever so sorry to hear about your son.

Eden   Well . . . thank . . . (*Pause.*) War, it . . . Everybody lost somebody.

Clarissa (*beat. Smiles*)   I thought you were an actor, actually. The first time we met.

Eden   Really?

Clarissa   You have that look. Like Errol Flynn.

Eden   Is that a good thing?

Clarissa   I think so. (*Pause.*) So they say one day you may be Prime Minister.

Eden   Well. That's . . . Hmm. (*Pause.*) You know I, uh . . . have recently . . . divorced . . .

Clarissa   Yes, I did know that. Though I hardly see why it matters.

Eden   It does to some.

Clarissa   Well, they're silly.

Eden   You *are* a Roman Catholic.

Clarissa   I'm also a woman. (*Pause.*) Why did she . . . leave?

Eden   Uh, it all got a little . . . much. Politics wasn't in her blood. Alas. I . . . well. Don't blame her. (*Pause.*) Would it bother you?

Clarissa   I'm a Churchill, Anthony. It *is* my blood.

They smile as they dance into a racier jitterbug, opening out to become less formal, more sensual and fun.

They disappear as **Reporter** *and* **Caricaturist** *appear.*

Reporter   Course, that one's getting in with the old boy's niece, now. That won't do him any harm in the long run, will it?

Caricaturist   No. So long as he doesn't stray this time.

Reporter   Stray, Fred?

Caricaturist   Well, you know. Good-looking. Powerful. He's uh . . . well. Made good use of his talents, Bill, is all.

Clarissa's *home.*

Eden   Here. Uh, as a present, you know.

Clarissa   Oh, lovely. How kind. We're having fish, if that's all right. Busy day?

Eden   Uh, yes. So-so. Met with the Shadow Cabinet. At the Savoy, no less. And you?

Clarissa   Oh, just in the garden. And how was Uncle? His usual self?

Eden   'Fraid so. Though at least we've managed to get him out of bed now. (*Sighs.*) I'm sorry, I know he's family, but –

Clarissa   Gosh, you needn't fret. I know more than most how difficult he can be.

Eden   It's just all so gloomy and, worse, reactionary. I mean look what Labour are doing? A 'National Health Service'. State education for all. Us? There's no vision, no drive. Just moaning about the pettiest things. If it's not about those 'young Labour scallywags' coming onto our side of the Commons dining hall, it's how the opposition offices aren't as clean, or whatever, before Winston starts grumbling into his cream tea with a torrent of inconsequential ramblings, and then, lo!, we're back on the War again! (*Taking his glass of wine.*) It's a pain in the neck, it really is.

Clarissa   Anthony, calm down. You just need to be stronger. Firmer. Take off your shoes.

Eden   And they just go on and on, it's so tiresome. Seems all Tories have this irksome habit of starting a conversation without a point, hoping to find one along the way. And to keep jabbering on until one finds one! God!

Clarissa   Anthony. (*Taking his glass.*) Stop it. I will not waste good wine on a bad mood.

Eden   It's my wine.

Clarissa   No, it's not, you said it was a present. Now buck up, all right?

Eden   All right. Sorry. (*Taking the glass of wine.*) Sometimes I just despair of the whole wretched thing. As much as Rab, Harold and I try to push us forward, it's no good until we get rid of all these old dinosaurs on our front bench.

Clarissa   One in particular.

Eden *pauses.*

Clarissa   Does he mention it often?

Eden   Others do. I don't know. Wish he'd never labelled me as next in line. Crown Prince is hardly an enviable position. And he talks continually as though he is anointed by God. The time he was walking through London during the blitz, and a bomb hits a building nearby. Everyone but Winston hits the ground. Asked why he wasn't afraid, he points up and says, 'He has not done with me yet.' How can you argue with that?

Clarissa   Well, your support in the party is unanimous.

Eden   How do you know?

Clarissa   Being a former Prime Minister's niece, you'd be surprised how many conversations one can find oneself within earshot of.

Eden (*pause*)   You know he first mentioned my succession back in '42. That long ago. A secret between us. Now everyone knows and it's just unbearable. I could take the party forward, and the country, I know it, I *know* it. But every time we broach the subject we end up rowing. We really are turning into father and son!

Clarissa   And when we're married, he really will be family.

Eden   God, don't remind me! His control over me will be final. (*Pause.*) 'Uncle Winston'.

They laugh.

Clarissa   You know, for the honeymoon I was thinking Portugal or France? Any thoughts?

Eden   Well, it rather depends what happens here. With the election.

Clarissa   I don't see how. We will be going on a honeymoon, Anthony.

Eden   I know.

Clarissa   We will.

Eden   Yes, I know. (*Pause.*) Speaking of the election. Played around with a new name today. Can you believe?

Clarissa   For what? The Conservatives?

Eden   Yes. The 'New Democrats'.

Clarissa   Ha! And what did Uncle say to that?

Eden   Said it sounded (*Mock-Winston voice.*) 'Nazi'. So there you go.

Clarissa   Oh, you're no Hitler, darling. Your moustache is much more charming. (*Kisses him.*) I don't know how that Eva Braun put up with the wretched thing tickling her.

Eden (*serious*)   Don't joke, darling.

Clarissa (*pause*)   Well, you know if you need help on the campaign trail . . .

Eden   Thank you. That's awfully kind.

Clarissa   It's what Beatrice did for you. Last time. Wasn't it?

Eden (*pause*)   Yes. Though that's by the by. You shouldn't . . . shouldn't feel you must –

Clarissa   I know. I'm only doing it for a place in the Cabinet once you're PM.

Eden   Certainly. How does Minister of Fish and Wine grab you?

Clarissa   Perfect.

They kiss.

An explosion of sound as lights pick up **Churchill** *at a podium, cheering and waving, giving the V-sign to his adoring public. Cheering and clapping. Red white and blue ticker tape falls around him, as 'Jerusalem' plays, and we move into* **Churchill***'s quarters. He is with* **Eden***.*

Churchill   We're back, Anthony! Back!

Eden   Congratulations, Winston.

Churchill   And now to the matter in hand. As to who goes where and what and why. So, I must formally ask you, Mr Eden, if you would do me the honour of taking over . . . at the Foreign Office again.

Eden (*pause, then visibly deflated*)   Right.

Churchill   My Anthony. Your time will come, I promise you that. I shall hand over power before the end of this parliament.

Eden (*still dejected*)   Right.

Churchill   The world is still weak and the cure slow. The War left Britain skinny and poor and in the pockets of those who had not fought for so long or so hard. I need the best Foreign Secretary I have. And you are the finest international negotiator there is. So go and join the leaders of this world. For Britain, Anthony. And be strong . . .

He disappears.

Three independent places appear in pools of light:

PARIS   *Two armchairs.* **Schuman** *reclines in one. A small table with two glasses of wine. Cigar smoke. The French flag flies.*

CAIRO   *Two armchairs.* **Nasser** *reclines in one. On the table are two cups of Moroccan tea. Cigar smoke. The Egyptian flag flies.*

WASHINGTON   *Two armchairs.* **Dulles** *reclines in one. On the table are two cups of coffee. Cigar smoke. The American flag flies.*

The tango theme sounds as **Eden** *enters Paris, greeting* **Schuman** *in a dance hold, spinning into a seated position. The music fades down but remains in the background.*

Schuman   Well, what a welcome back for you, Mr Eden. A standing ovation from the United Nations Assembly!

Eden   The polite reception was most welcome, thank you.

Schuman   So. Mr Churchill was not available?

Eden   I am trusted with all foreign affairs, Monsieur Schuman. And I trust we can make steady progress today. So. You're not happy.

Schuman   I'm a politician.

Eden   You want Britain to go further. Be more committed to Europe publicly. I can understand that. But I'm afraid we cannot cast our net that far out as yet.

Schuman   I'm under pressure, you see. To show them something . . . real. What we are trying to create is a Community. You know, the geographical position of nations is something we cannot help. This is where we have been put, next to each other, and nothing we can do. Like the family you are born into. You cannot choose the sisters and the brothers that share your house. But you must do all that you can to live with them in a manner that is . . . mutually beneficial. Europe? Europe is not a land mass, a piece of earth. Europe is a state of mind. An idea, existing nowhere but in our head until ink lands on a dotted line. Until we have clear participants. Words, these words you offer, 'association', 'support'. They have no currency, nothing to hold in your hand and say 'there'. Britain is part of Europe's family, Mr Eden. We're just asking you to come and sit at the dinner table.

Eden   Our position is that we support a European Defence Community, but that our support would rather be . . . helping from the outside, rather than participating within.

Schuman   Ha! And once again, Britain's political position in Europe is also its geographical one. Looking from the outside in.

Eden   That is my position and the position of Her Majesty's Government. (*Standing.*) One moment, please.

Schuman   Remember. The Channel is only large in terms of psychology. In actual size, though, anyone who truly wanted to cross it could.

Schuman *and Paris fade slightly.*

Eden (*aside*)   You never managed it.

The tango theme rises as **Eden** *cross-steps over to Cairo and* **Nasser**. *They greet in a similar fashion, spinning to their seats as the tango fades again.*

Nasser   Where did you learn Arabic, Mr Eden?

Eden   At Oxford. Wonderful language. I find it has opened up a range of simply . . . uh, simply marvellous texts that would have otherwise been closed to me. The Koran, particularly, contains a great deal of wisdom. So. Have you made any decision on joining our Baghdad Pact? We have Iraq and Turkey now. Britain views Middle Eastern defence amongst its top priorities.

Nasser   And why is this?

Eden   Well. We have a . . . responsibility.

Nasser   We were pleased to finally settle the Base Agreement. The people of Egypt are looking forward with hope to the end of British occupation.

Eden   Occupation? Colonel Nasser, I hardly . . .

Nasser   Despite the declaration of independence, what, thirty years ago? We still find ourselves at British mercy.

Eden   No Egyptian citizen is at our mercy and I really must object to such a statement.

Nasser   I'm sorry. (*Smiles.*) My English is perhaps not translating as it should.

Eden   Yes, perhaps not. But this all seems rather academic now, anyway. The treaty has been signed. Our forces will be out within two years. Including the Suez Canal Zone.

Nasser (*pause*)   Where is Mr Churchill? I was hoping to meet with him.

Eden   Well, he isn't here. You'll be dealing with me.

Nasser   Hmm.

Pause. Cairo and **Nasser** *fade slightly. The tango theme rises.* **Eden** *crosses to Washington and greets* **Dulles** *with a similar flourish and sits. The tango quietens.*

Dulles   I never really got a chance to, uh . . . congratulate your negotiating prowess on Iran, Anthony. Seems you were right about Mussadeq after all. I think it's safe to say we'll all benefit now he's gone. And forty per cent of the oil revenue! Well done, you.

Eden   Well. A victory for peace is a victory for all, Mr Dulles. And we all have a, uh . . . a responsibility towards peace, now.

Dulles   It was a shame we didn't quite see eye to eye when it mattered in Geneva, though. We feel it's important to keep a united front, especially when sitting across the table from the Russians and Chinese. Particularly when it comes to Germany and Europe.

Eden   I've no doubt that we will only ever differ on the details, Foster. Britain's desired outcomes for peace and international security will always be the same as yours.

Churchill's *hand extends out from the darkness to tap* **Eden** *on the shoulder.*

Eden   Would you excuse me, please?

Washington and **Dulles** *dim. The tango theme ceases completely.* **Churchill** *appears.*

Churchill   Anthony. What is the worst thing that could happen to us? (*Pause.*) The King is dead. Princess Elizabeth is flying back from her tour to become our new Queen.

Eden   Heavens. (*Beat. Laughs faintly, shrugging.*) God save the . . . Queen.

Churchill   Of course, I shouldn't think I could leave any time soon, now. Must get our new monarch settled in first, what? Then we'll talk about a transfer of power.

Eden   Um. Yes. (*Sighs.*) Right . . .

Churchill *disappears as the tango music sounds.* **Eden** *spins back to Washington.*

Dulles   What is it with the English and tea? Personally, I think it tastes like dirty water. Have to put five sugars in it to get any goddamn taste. Now coffee is a real drink.

Eden   Well. Tea will always be the choice of England.

Dulles   We'll see. (*Sips.*) You know, the United States have their own issues too, Anthony. With Europe, frankly, we feel we've done all we can. And God knows we've given as much financial assistance as possible before we cripple ourselves. We're not a charity, Mr Eden. Didn't we come to your aid when you needed it?

Eden   Of course. Of which we will be for ever in your debt. We were certainly worn out after fighting for so long. Alone. But we couldn't just allow tyranny to spread across the globe unchecked, now could we? Apathy and Evil go hand in hand.

Washington and **Dulles** *dim, the tango rises, as* **Eden** *crosses to Paris. Tango quietens.*

Eden   You talk of family. That's nice. Our problem is we've so many responsibilities elsewhere. Commitments to the Commonwealth, they're our *immediate* family, now NATO, the UN. Our special relationship with the United States –

Schuman   Uh-hum. *Entente Cordiale?*

Eden   And with the French.

Schuman (*beat, then smiles and toasts*)   *Merci.*

Eden   We certainly wouldn't be prepared to commit to the EDC without the integration of Germany. They must be actively involved. At least one division in any federal army.

Schuman   That would mean rearming them.

Eden   We don't have a problem with that.

Schuman   You don't live next door.

Eden   We must learn from the mistakes of Versailles. We believe in second chances.

Schuman   Yes. Well. This would be their third.

Eden   One regiment can't start a war.

Schuman   In 1939, one man did! (*Pause.*) Look, if we let everyone into this community then we won't need defending from anyone anyway.

Eden   I rather thought that was the point.

Schuman   We need signed confirmation of your assistance in the event of any aggression.

Eden   Do you really think, Monsieur, that Britain would not come to the aid of France, or anyone, under attack? Have we not always, our fathers, grandfathers, our . . . sons, defended those in need? Whether there is or is not a piece of paper saying we have to?

Paris and **Schuman** *dim, tango rises, as* **Eden** *crosses to Washington. Tango quietens.*

Dulles   Say, where *is* Churchill?

Beat. **Eden** *grimaces as the tango rises and he crosses to Cairo, where it fades.*

Nasser   And I would like to give congratulations on your new Queen. You do not mind being led by a lady? (*Laughs.*)

Eden   In our history, the Queens have generally been more ferocious than the Kings. But, yes, it was a huge success. Watched on television by millions, no less.

Nasser   Astonishing! This new thing of tele . . . television. Still, it is not all so good for the people to see so much into the government working. In Egypt, I think we will not let them see so much. They might find things they do not like.

Eden   Well, in Britain, all documents must eventually become public property. We're even looking into reducing the embargo to just fifty years before information is released.

Nasser   What a thing!

Clarissa*'s hand appears from the darkness to tap him on the shoulder.*

Eden   Please, ex . . . one moment . . .

Cairo and **Nasser** *dim. The tango theme ceases.*

Clarissa *appears.*

Clarissa   Winston's had a stroke. He's fine, but . . . well . . . taking it easy.

Eden   Oh. Uh . . . heavens. Right. Well.

Clarissa   Anthony, are you all right? You look exhausted. Maybe *you* should see someone.

Eden   No, of course not. I'm fine. And busy. Excuse me.

Eden *returns to Cairo and* **Nasser** *with a brief burst of the tango theme.*

Nasser   Yet, the Base Agreement allows you to reoccupy the Suez Canal when you please.

Eden   Only in an emergency. Should the free passage of the Canal come under threat. As . . . as the nation that built it and owns it, Britain has a certain responsibility to ensure free passage for the entire world. And we don't take that role lightly.

Nasser   The free passage is safeguarded by the 1888 convention. Egypt will always respect that. Except with Israel, of course! Another Western conquest, carved deep into the heart of Palestine. It seems wherever we find tension in the Middle East, Mr Eden, we find the British Empire.

Pause. **Eden** *leaves Cairo in a burst of tango music, crossing into Washington.*

Dulles   Of course you're right, Anthony. Though Europe really needs to learn to stand on its own two feet. My people, we're . . . well, we're shifting our focus. To Asia. The Middle East. Keep that ticking over.

Eden (*mopping his brow*)   And the oil flowing.

Dulles   Foreign aid costs money, Anthony. And. Well. We now see ourselves as liberators. Heroes of the downtrodden and the oppressed. Fighters for those who want independence from Empire.

Eden   Careful. You'll be taking *our* territories away next.

Dulles   We've made no secret of our dislike for colonialism and your imperialist past, Mr Eden. Let's not forget that we were once in your grasp. We were, of course, happy to see you finally let India go. And that you're withdrawing from Palestine. Egypt.

Eden   Yes, we were less pleased to hear of your arms package to Colonel Nasser. Do you really think that's wise? To a fast-becoming fiery, nationalist dictator?

Dulles   Don't take offence, Anthony. Like you say, we are living in a different world. No longer can we afford to float around, oblivious to anything outside our own borders.

Eden   We . . . (*Holding his side and wincing.*) We never did.

Dulles   Are you all right?

Clarissa'*s hand appears from the darkness, tapping* **Eden** *on the shoulder.*

Eden   Would you . . . one second, please.

Washington and **Dulles** *dim. The tango ceases completely.*

Clarissa *appears.*

Clarissa   Anthony, the doctors would like to do some tests. You're not well.

Eden   You don't understand.

Clarissa   You're working yourself into the grave, do *you* understand? You need a break!

Eden   I can't stop now. Winston . . . all that I've . . . I'll lose my chance, damn it! I'm fine!

Clarissa *disappears as the tango bursts out.* **Eden** *crosses, holding his side, to Paris. The tango quietens. He appears to cover his pain quite well.*

Schuman   We will have to settle with that for now, then. *Bien. (Drinks.)* I must congratulate you on your new wife. She is well?

Eden   Uh . . . yes, yes she's – we're . . . thank you, we're both well.

Schuman   And your boss? You must be getting really eager to take over now, yes?

Eden   You . . . shouldn't pay attention to gossip, Monsieur Schuman. Our house is in order.

Schuman *(laughing)*   Things have not changed, have they? Since your Henry VIII or our Louis XIV. We still find ourselves at the mercy of the gossip and treachery of the court!

Paris and **Schuman** *disappear, a quick burst of tango as* **Eden** *stumbles to Cairo.*

Eden   President, I'm sure . . . I'm sure you appreciate that the Canal is an international asset, vital for world trade. And, if you recall, the . . . the 1936 treaty granted Her Majesty's Government certain base rights and was, once again, I stress, agreed by your predecessors. Not only to protect our citizens here but to act as a force of stability in the region as a whole against . . . rising tensions. Another reason why we were hoping for your inclusion in the Baghdad Pact.

Nasser *(pause. Serious)*   When I became president, I vowed that my people would once again be free from the rule of Empire. And, at last, this is happening. I really do not see the need for an imperial Western power to / construct a treaty of alliance –

Eden   Imperial Western power?

Nasser   – between our Arab neighbours. This is something we should be doing for ourselves. We will not be joining your pact, Mr Eden.

Eden   Well you . . . I must confess –

Nasser   But enjoy the rest of your stay as guests in my country. As guests, you understand.

Eden   Well you, you . . . yes, I . . . just –

Cairo and **Nasser** *disappear. A burst of tango as* **Eden** *collapses over to Washington.* **Dulles** *embraces him in a dance hold to steady him, and to lead him to his seat.*

Dulles   Course, now there's NATO. There's the United Nations.

Eden   Yes, of . . . uh . . .

Dulles   Other people's affairs, well . . . it's not only our responsibility now, but also our *right* to intervene when and where we see fit. And truth be told . . . well, truth be told, we've opened our eyes since the War. And what we see is a lot to be done. And to that end, Mr Eden, my country . . . well, like I say. Europe, we're nearly done with. Now we're looking . . .

Dr Hume'*s hand appears out from the darkness to tap* **Eden** *on the shoulder.*

Dulles (*smiling*) . . . further afield.

Washington and **Dulles** *and the scene disappear. The tango ends.* **Dr Hume** *appears.*

Dr Hume   Foreign Secretary. I . . . I'm afraid the results have come back from your test and it's, uh . . . not all good. We've found gallstones in your bile duct, and . . . well, we should need to operate immediately.

Eden   Well I . . . I . . . I really am – I'm rather busy at the moment, you know, and –

Dr Hume   Oh, don't worry. It was partly the Prime
Minister's suggestion you take some time off. In fact, he's all
for it.

Eden (*beat*)   Really? That so?

Dr Hume   And he's impressed upon me how, uh . . . well,
how damn important you are. Kept telling me about the time –

Churchill *appears, barking in their direction.*

Churchill   I had my appendix cut out of me with a bread
knife on the kitchen table. Bah! You'll be fine, man. I shall
make sure this chap knows exactly how important you are.

Operating theatre. **Dr Hume** *in a small pool of light, wielding a
scalpel, looking down at a body covered in a white sheet. The beat of a
heart monitor.* **Dr Hume** *looks around nervously before lowering the
knife and beginning to cut. Suddenly, a red patch of blood begins forming
underneath the white blanket. The beat of the heart monitor increases.*
Dr Hume *begins to panic, his hands working away under the blanket,
the level of blood swelling, as the heart monitor beats at a faster rate.
Blackout.*

Dr Hume *with* **Eden**, *who looks ill and very weak.*

Eden   What . . . do you mean?

Dr Hume   The knife. It just, um . . . slipped I'm afraid. And
we . . . accidentally . . . severed your bile duct. (*Pause.*) Sorry.

Churchill *appears.* **Dr Hume** *disappears.*

Churchill   Well, I was going to set a deadline for the transfer
of power, Anthony. But I can't very well expect you to take
over now. The doctors think it will kill you. And I cannot have
that. You need to get fit, Anthony. Fit and well. Then we'll
talk.

Silence. **Churchill** *disappears as* **Eden** *spins angrily into:*

Eden *and* **Clarissa***'s apartment, Carlton Gardens.* **Eden** *slams his hat onto the floor.*

Eden   THAT INSUFFERABLE OLD FOOL!

He grabs his side in pain. **Clarissa** *goes to him, lowering him to a chair.*

Eden   I'm fine!

Clarissa   You are not fine, you need to rest. / Sit back.

Eden   My life has been resting, and waiting, and sitting back, and *waiting*!

Clarissa   That's not true.

Eden   It was him! Put the fear of death into the surgeon. Be on drugs now for the rest of my . . . Cholangitis of the liver, now! So there you are! Go in with one, come out with a-bloody-nother. The kiss of death, that's what he . . . 'Heir Apparent'. Nothing 'apparent' about it. Positively indistinct! The life of the understudy! (*Sighs.*) We had a deal. And I swear he's taunting me with it! At the American dinner today, he's looking over the garden at Number 10 with the President and he says − knowing I can hear − that he's thinking of cutting down the poplars so he can see the Trooping of the Colour properly . . . *next year*! So I end up storming over to him and yelling that they weren't his to cut down. And he just smiled. Lord knows what Eisenhower thought. And Cabinet's a mess, no one believes he knows what he's doing any more. Selwyn Lloyd's positive the only reason he's in the Foreign Office is because Winston thought he was *Geoffrey* Lloyd, and then couldn't be bothered with the paperwork to sort it out, and Walter Elliot missed out on the Cabinet because he was out of the house when Winston telephoned! Answer in three rings or you're out! That silly old man!

Clarissa   Oh Anthony, you shouldn't let him get to you so.

Eden   Reminds me of Eton when everyone in the years above were going off to war except me. The *first* war. (*Beat.*) And my housemaster there was called Churchill!

Clarissa   Never.

Eden   Would you believe it?! Probably part of the same bloody family! No offence. (*Pause.*) Said I had too soft a heart for war. Whilst all around me, friends left to fight.

Clarissa   Well, you proved them wrong, darling. Men with soft hearts don't fight their way into the trenches and win a Military Cross, do they?

Eden   For what it's worth. My sons fighting the same enemies years later. Only . . . not being so fortunate.

Clarissa   Oh, Anthony, stop.

Eden   I just want the chance to . . . make things better. And I could. I could! Given the chance I . . . I could. Heal old wounds.

Clarissa   Well, you need to get yourself better first. (*Softly, stroking his hair.*) And I'm afraid there are some wounds that politics can't heal.

Eden (*pause*)   It was the waiting. Huh. (*Shakes his head.*) Again! Waiting . . . for news, after his plane went down. Nothing . . . nothing prepares you. (*Pause.*) Amongst, uh . . . Simon's things, they . . . in the wreckage, found a copy of . . . *Henry V.* (*Smiles.*) Kept up with his . . . just as I told him. And all the others, countless others who . . . never came . . . (*Bitterly.*) 'Once more unto the breach, dear friends, once more! Or close . . . (*Calmer.*) . . . close the wall up with our . . . English dead.' (*Tries to compose himself.*) They say the . . . the hardest thing a man has to do is . . . is bury his son. I think, though . . . *not* being able to bury him . . . is . . . is probably . . . far worse . . .

Clarissa *embraces him as he collapses into her. Lights fade.*

Churchill *appears in his quarters, sitting at his desk. His head leans to one side, as though asleep. For a time, all that can be heard is his heavy, rhythmic breathing, which sounds painful and wheezing. Half his face is slightly paralysed from a stroke. Footsteps from the darkness.* **Harold Macmillan** *enters.* **Churchill** *looks up.*

Churchill   Mr Macmillan.

Macmillan   Good evening, Prime Minister.

Churchill   H-how are things in Housing, Harold, with all your success?

Macmillan   We're building on it all the time.

They both chuckle politely. Pause.

Winston. We'd like to talk about your succession.

Churchill   W . . . we?

Butler *enters.*

Butler   Yes, Prime Minister. Wondered if you had any thoughts.

Macmillan   You did say you wouldn't fight another election. And we're going to need someone else in as soon as possible. Leave them enough time to build a campaign.

Churchill   Yes, well, it's . . . all very well to say . . . to say we'd like, we need. But it is a . . . a matter of choosing the best time.

Butler   What we need is an anniversary or something. An 'apt' time for a change. 'This many years' in power, or 'so many' as leader, that kind of thing.

Churchill   But the climate, gentlemen. The, the conditions.

Swinton *enters.*

Swinton   How about your eightieth birthday, Prime Minister? That might be an apt time.

Churchill   My . . . ? (*Pause.*) Yes, perhaps you're . . . (*Unsure.*) Yes.

Woolton *enters.* **Churchill** *is now practically encircled.*

Woolton   And then there's the matter of your successor.

Churchill   Well you . . . you know who my successor is to be. Anthony.

Swinton (*pause*)   Yes . . .

Churchill   Can you think of anyone better?

Woolton   Well – (*Indicating.*) Rab of course. And Harold.

Swinton   Personally I think anybody would be better. His health, for a start. And he can never seem to make up his mind, which doesn't bode well. And his temperament!

Butler   Let's not forget this is the man once considered to become the first ever Secretary General of the UN. He's a proven diplomat and an accomplished politician. And he's been in line for the throne for over a decade.

Woolton   Well, exactly. There's no point in arguing now. What's done is done.

Churchill   Harold?

Macmillan   I trust in your opinion, Prime Minister.

Churchill   Well. You'll have to have him.

Macmillan (*pause*)   When?

Butler, Swinton, Woolton *and* **Macmillan** *disappear.*

Eden *enters to stand in front of* **Churchill***. Silence, punctured by* **Churchill***'s wheezing, as they stare at each other.*

Churchill   He . . . is almost done with me, Anthony. I have been possessed . . . my entire life . . . by the history I was making. Time now . . . to raise the white flag. A *stroke* . . . of good fortune for you. 'Unto whomsoever much is given . . . of him . . . much shall be required.' Remember. Indecision is a most fatal vice. Better act wrongly but quickly . . . than lose the chance of acting at all. I have not chosen you, Anthony. History has chosen you. You will find out . . . soon enough . . . why . . .

Elgar's 'Nimrod' creeps in as the lights around **Churchill** *slowly die.*

Eden *steps onto a podium. Hung there is a poster emblazoned with the 1955 Tory Party election slogan, 'Working for Peace', as the hubbub of crowds and horns grows to become deafening.*

Eden   My government will be one of efficiency and fair play. My Britain will be one of strong industry and manufacture, a happy employer and a happy workforce. I have fought all my life for Britain abroad. Now, at a momentous moment in the history of not only our country but our world, when there is not a single war in progress recorded anywhere on the surface of the earth, I am ready to fight for her at home!

The cheers and 'Jerusalem' explode. **Clarissa** *joins the waving* **Eden** *on the podium as a shower of ticker tape engulfs them, lit up by the flash of camera bulbs.*

Downing Street. Prime Minister's chambers. Desk, British flag, portrait of the Queen. **Eden** *alone.* **Bishop** *enters and shakes his hand.*

Bishop   Prime Minister.

Eden   Yes. Yes, I believe I am. Pleasure, Mr Bishop.

Bishop   It is an honour to serve as your Private Secretary.

Eden   Thank you, Fred.

Bishop   Mr Harold Macmillan.

Macmillan *appears.*

Eden   Harold. How does the Foreign Office grab you?

Macmillan (*pause*)   Very nicely. Prime Minister.

Eden   I've kept it nice and warm for you, eh?

Macmillan   Thank you.

Macmillan *disappears.* **Lloyd** *appears.*

Bishop   Mr Selwyn Lloyd.

Eden   Selwyn. Fancy a go at Defence?

Lloyd   Why the devil not? Thank you, Anthony.

Lloyd *disappears.* **Anthony Nutting** *appears.*

Bishop Mr Anthony Nutting. Junior Minister at the Foreign Office.

Eden Of course. Nice to keep you on board, Mr Nutting.

Nutting The pleasure is all mine, Prime Minister. You've been a great role model to me.

Eden Well. Your work in Egypt over the Base Agreement was commendable. Keep it up.

Nutting I shan't let you down.

Eden If I've learnt anything, Mr Nutting, it is to conduct foreign affairs with the utmost integrity, gentlemanly conduct and never, never, make it personal.

Nutting *disappears.* **Clarissa** *appears.*

Bishop Lady Clarissa Eden. Your wife.

Bishop *exits.*

Clarissa *takes off some gardener's gloves she's wearing*

Clarissa (*beaming*) 'Prime Minister'.

Eden Ma'am.

A beat. **Clarissa** *skips excitedly over and kisses him on the cheek as they hug tight.*

Eden (*laughing*) How do you like your new home, darling?

Clarissa Suits me fine, thank you. Just fine. Though the garden has been practically reclaimed by nature. Lot of dirty work to be done.

Eden For both of us.

Clarissa I hear Winston is on the mend and feeling better now.

Eden (*beat, fearfully*) Well, I'm here now, we've moved in all our things.

Clarissa (*laughing*)   Oh darling, I meant nothing by it. Silly thing. (*Looking at the portrait of the Queen.*) She has asked you to serve her, Anthony. Just don't forget. She is not the only woman in your life . . . who needs you.

Prime Minister's chambers. **Eden** *is pacing, reading his notes.* **Bishop** *is listening.*

Eden   . . . 'Strikes overcome through' . . . (*Scribbles.*) 'as a result of this government's partnership with industry.' (*Writes.*) 'Succeed in building three hundred thousand houses, a sustainable . . . a sustainable growth our', uh . . . (*Scribbles, then sighs.*) Gad, why do I find speaking to the House so fiendishly terrifying?

Bishop   You always do fine, Prime Minister. You know, Winston used to take six hours practising his speeches.

Eden   Hmm.

Bishop   It will be Gaitskell who is terrified today. It's his first time at the Labour helm. You should just play the 'new opposition leader appealing to the middle ground just to make his party electable again' card. That ought to do it.

Eden   Ye-es. (*With a newspaper.*) You know, it's being touted that I am weak at the despatch box, Fred. Have you seen this? 'To emphasise a point he will clash one fist to smash the open palm of the other, but the smash is seldom heard!' I mean really!

Bishop   You shouldn't pay so much attention to the press, Prime Minister. The country rates you / as highly popular.

Eden   Seldom heard! I ask you. (*Smacks his hand with the other.*) You can hear that, can't you? Trying to make me the laughing stock of Whitehall. And what is the talk in the smoking room? Any consensus so far?

Bishop   You needn't worry, Prime Minister.

Eden (*pause*)   How do you think Harold is faring at the Foreign Office? Good choice?

Bishop I believe fine, Prime Minister.

Eden Hmm. I'll telegram Menzies. Get word from the other side of the world, yes?

Bishop I could notify the Foreign Office on your behalf?

Eden No, that's all right. I'll do it. I should see how the preparations for the Commonwealth Conference are going anyway.

Bishop May I make a suggestion, Prime Minister?

Eden Yes, go on.

Bishop I think you can rely on your officials to keep their eyes on overseas. All that's being handled by someone else now.

Eden (*pause*) Yes, of . . . no, of course. Just a, uh . . . few little aches for my old job, you know. But you're right. After facing out to the rest of the world for so long, time to turn around and face in a little more, eh?

Bishop Quite right. Let someone else fret about that silly little Commonwealth.

Eden I beg your pardon?

Bishop Just a little joke, Prime Minister.

Eden Well, don't. They are our family, Bishop. And one must always respect one's family. They make Britain more than the sum of its parts. We are their parents. Not so long ago, our influence spread across a third of the world. But alas, like all children . . . they're growing up. And leaving home. (*Facing the Queen's portrait.*) They don't need us any more, Fred. One day we shall be left this island alone. (*Pause.*) Do you know I familiarised myself with all our possessions by heart, Fred?

Bishop Really?

Eden Oh yes. My duty, you know. And something to do on all those flights everywhere.

Bishop How many is that, sir?

Eden   Eight in the Commonwealth. Then forty other territories, protectorates and such.

Bishop   And you know them all by heart?

Eden (*pause. Smiles*)   You don't believe me.

Bishop   Of course, Prime –

Eden   Canada, Australia, New Zealand, South Africa, India, Pakistan, Ceylon, United Kingdom.

Bishop   Very good, Prime –

Eden   Then we have, well . . . Gibraltar, Malta, Singapore. Hong Kong. Uh . . . Zanzibar. The Seychelles. Jamaica. Maybe you should be writing these down.

Bishop   I, I'm sorry?

Eden   I'm saying maybe you should be writing these down. So we don't say the same ones twice. (*Pause.*) Come along.

Bishop (*pause. He takes a pad and pencil from his pocket*)   Sir.

Eden   Canada, Australia, New Zealand . . .

Westminster. Press room.

Caricaturist (*sketching on a pad*)   So. How do you think the old boy's doing, then?

Reporter (*writing. Sipping coffee*)   All right. Storming the polls, ain't he?

Caricaturist   Oh yeah. But then they always do the first year, don't they?

Reporter   Mm. Good campaign though, I thought.

Caricaturist   Did yer?

Reporter   Yes, I did. Fought like a gentleman.

Caricaturist   Oh yeah. Then he always was one of those, wasn't he?

Reporter   One of those?

Caricaturist   One of them. Born into it and all that. Eton.

Reporter   Oh yeah. Money.

Caricaturist   Buy yourself into it, can't you?

Reporter   Hmm.

Caricaturist   Pay for it. I could have been a gentleman if my old man had paid for me to be one.

Reporter   You are a gentleman, Fred.

Caricaturist   Ah. Thank you, Bill. So are you.

Downing Street. Prime Minister's chambers.

Eden   . . . Tanganyika. Uh, Swaziland. Bermuda. How many's that?

Bishop   That's thirty-eight.

Eden (*pause*)   Hong Kong?

Bishop   You've had that one, I'm afraid.

Eden   Don't be pedantic, Bishop. (*Pause.*) Kenya! Kenya!

Bishop (*writing*)   Kenya.

Eden   Good old Kenya. (*Pause.*) How many's that?

Bishop   You need one more, Prime Minister.

Eden   Are you sure? (*Pause.*) Damn it man, one more.

Bishop   If it's any consolation, that's pretty impressive off the top of your head, sir.

Eden   No, no it's not. I know them all. (*Takes the pad.*)

Bishop   Well, I'm afraid your audience with the Queen will be starting shortly, Prime Minister. We'll need to be getting you to the palace.

Eden   Fine, fine. (*Gathering some files and making to leave.*) But this isn't over.

Bishop   Perhaps Her Majesty could help.

Eden (*barking as he exits*)   I don't need any help!

Downing Street. Bedroom. **Eden** *in bed has a telephone on his lap, the receiver rested on his cheek and shoulder, notes on his lap.* **Clarissa** *lies next to him, reading.*

Eden (*on the phone*)   Ah, Harold. Yes. Now. (*Pause.*) Sorry? (*Pause.*) Yes, I'm aware of that, Harold. I just have a few amendments to your Iranian telegram. (*Pause.*) No, it's fine, I just . . . (*Pause.*) This part where you say – are you writing this down? (*Pause.*) Well you *should* keep a pencil by your bed, I do. (*Pause.*) Oh, listen, go and get one, I'll call you back. (*Pause.*) No, don't put me onto . . . Hello Dorothy. (*Pause.*) Yes, I do apologise. (*Sighs. Pause.*) Yes, w-would you like to speak to Clarissa?

Clarissa *shoots him a look, shaking her head.*

Eden   Look, can – I'll call back in a minute. Tha – ye – bye. (*Replacing the receiver.*) God, that man. He thinks every bloody telegram he writes is as sacred as the Bible.

Clarissa   You wouldn't have stood for Uncle Winston rewriting yours. You need to be careful, Anthony. You don't want a reputation as one who –

Eden   What?

Clarissa   Fusses.

Eden   It is a Prime Minister's duty to fuss. The bigger picture is made up of the minutiae.

Clarissa   Learn to trust your officials, Anthony. It's better for them and it's certainly better for you. And you're getting a cold.

Eden   Just a runny nose.

Clarissa   That's the first sign.

Eden   Not if all you've got is a runny nose, then it's the last sign.

Clarissa   You need to wrap up more. If Dr Evans saw you he'd have a fit. You should wear your homburg.

Eden   I do wear my homburg.

Clarissa   It's cold. You'll catch your death.

Eden   Well, what? Do you want me to wear it now, should I put it on now?

Clarissa (*pause. Smiles*)   Yes.

Eden (*pause. Smiles back, wryly*)   All right.

He hops out of bed and exits the light.

Clarissa   What did he give you?

Eden (*off*)   Nothing. More Benzedrine. Help with my circulation.

He returns and gets back into bed, wearing his homburg. He poses mockingly, and **Clarissa** *laughs.*

Clarissa   What a handsome English gent you are!

Eden   Why, thank you. (*Going back to his notes.*) Anyway. Things will calm down now the Russian visit is over.

Clarissa   Until the next one. When is King Feisal coming to stay?

Eden *laughs.*

Clarissa   What? What's so funny?

Eden   Nothing. You . . . It's a state visit from the King of Iraq. You phrase it as though it were your mother coming over for the Bank Holiday.

Clarissa   Well, it's all the same, my mother or the King of Iraq. Still need to change the sheets, don't we? (*Pause.*) Well, we should get away after that. Somewhere warm. And quiet.

(*She curls up to him.*) Just you and me. No one else for miles and miles. Relaxing. On the beach. In our bathing outfits. And no telephone!

Eden   Well, I'll need a telephone, darling.

Clarissa   Not on the beach. (*Beat.*) I thought my outfit for the Russians was ghastly on reflection. Get one of your cronies to check what Her Majesty is wearing for this one. Make sure we don't clash.

Eden   I hardly think that's likely, darling.

Clarissa   Why not?

Eden   Just that . . . Nothing. (*Chuckles.*) I don't think she goes to the same shops.

Clarissa   What does that mean? She wears better clothes than me?

Eden   She wears different clothes from you. (*Dialling another number on the phone.*)

Clarissa   You think I'm going to embarrass you?

Eden   I think it's incredible I can negotiate international treaties with foreign dictators, yet I'm diplomatically impotent when it comes to a conversation with my wife.

Clarissa   I fancy Jamaica.

Eden   Send me a postcard. (*On the phone.*) Ah. Mrs Butler? (*Pause.*) Hello. Prime Minister here. Is your husband available? (*Pause.*) Well, be a dear. Give him a nudge.

Downing Street. **Eden** *with* **Bishop**. **Lloyd** *appears.*

Eden   Selwyn, old boy. Having a reshuffle. What do you say to the Foreign Office?

Lloyd (*nods*)   Prime Minister.

Lloyd *disappears.* **Macmillan** *appears.*

Eden   Harold. You're going to the Treasury. Congratulations. Chancellor of the Exchequer.

Macmillan (*pause*)   Thank you, Prime Minister.

Macmillan *disappears.* **Eden** *claps his hands together in a 'job well done' fashion.*

Eden   There.

Bishop   Prime Minister? Making Harold Chancellor. Such a . . . well, prominent man so close to the prize, as it were? (*Pause.*) Forgive my presumptions, Prime Minister.

Eden   Thank you, Fred. Suggestion noted.

Westminster. Press room. **Caricaturist** *is pulling 'toothy' faces as he sketches.*

Caricaturist   Quite 'toothy', Sir Anthony. Ain't he?

Reporter   See he's shuffling people around already. Butler. Lloyd. Macmillan.

Caricaturist   Hmm. All sounds very sensible to me, though, Bill.

Reporter   Do you think? (*Pause.*) So, lot more work for Mac, then. Less time to, uh . . . check on up his wife, if you know what I mean.

Caricaturist   I think there are plenty of gentlemen who know that, Bill. (*Laughs.*)

Reporter   Word is, Mac has heard that too. Course, he'll never leave her.

Caricaturist   Would you? (*Laughs.*) Why don't you, uh . . . you know. (*Gestures to the notepad.*) Slip something in. Quite a coup, wouldn't you say? That story?

Reporter   There are certain things one shouldn't 'report', Fred. A gentlemen's private life has no bearing on his integrity as a politician. And I rue the day when serious journalism becomes nothing more than grotesque gossip for the hoi polloi.

Caricaturist   Hmm. (*Glancing at his notepad.*) I'm thinking of giving Mac a forked tongue.

Downing Street. Prime Minister's chambers. **Eden** *is peeking through the window,* **Lloyd** *watching behind him.*

Eden   Ye gods, would you look at that man. It's as though he thinks being Chancellor makes him Elvis Presley. Loitering on the steps so they can get a better shot of him. I've made the wrong choice, haven't I?

Lloyd   You can't blame Harold, Anthony. We all do it.

Eden   I don't do it! Always waving, playing to the crowds. A small salute is enough for me. But him. Desperate to get a cheer. Course Winston was the worst. All he'd have to do was give the victory fingers and he'd have women fainting into the road. Though at least Winston had earned it.

Bishop *enters, followed by* **Macmillan**. **Eden** *continues at the window, unaware.*

Eden   What's this chap done? Flouncing around like he owns the place.

Macmillan   Who is this, Prime Minister?

Eden (*turning. Beat*)   Prince Philip. (*Pause.*) Can't stand the man.

Macmillan   Ah.

Eden (*pause*)   Don't tell him, will you?

Macmillan   Safe with me, Prime Minister.

Lloyd (*pause, then hastily*)   Right, we'll leave you to it, gentlemen.

Lloyd *and* **Bishop** *make a hasty exit. Silence.*

Eden   Your budget has been emphatically received, Harold. Despite a cut of one hundred million in expenditure, the press seem to like you.

Macmillan Yes, I don't know why, really. But I've never had it so good. (*Beat.*) Hmm . . .

Eden Hmm – yes. Well, all in all we haven't been producing enough. We're consuming too much of domestic production ourselves, leaving not enough to export.

Macmillan I've ordered the banks to reduce advances to customers. Local authorities are to cut back on spending . . .

Eden But despite world trade expanding at a healthy rate, Harold, Britain is scarcely managing to balance its payments. (*Facing the Queen's portrait.*) We're the fathers of industry, Harold. Architects of modern manufacture and commerce. Now everyone has caught up and is leaving us behind. How is a small island to cope? (*Mopping his brow.*)

Macmillan As it stands, our biggest expenditure is still defence.

Eden Well, withdrawal from Egypt is all but complete. Though we must keep on funding the atomic weapon research at Aldermaston. Cannot afford to be left behind there.

Macmillan And speaking of Egypt. Our finances are in place to fund the new Aswan Dam in the Nile. As are French and German. Any news from America?

Eden Mm. Dulles is giving the impression their enthusiasm is waning, given that Nasser keeps flip-flopping over the terms of the loan. God, he's getting to be bloody pain, that man. Lloyd rather suspects he was involved in Glubb's dismissal from Jordan as well.

Macmillan If the Americans withdraw their funding, the World Bank will do the same.

Eden Which will mean the end of the whole thing. Well. We'll keep an eye on it.

Downing Street. Prime Minister's chambers. **Eden**, **Bishop**,
Macmillan *and* **Lord Mountbatten** *sit having tea.*
Mountbatten *is dressed in naval officer's uniform.*

Eden   Bit of good news, Lord Mountbatten. The Jordanians
are joining the Baghdad pact.

Mountbatten   Well, that is good. Keep one foot in that
door, eh?

Macmillan   Yes, we rather thought it might be a good idea
to send them a present.

Eden   Ah. Yes. Now. Mr Lloyd and I were chatting about
this. Any thoughts?

Macmillan   Perhaps a fighter aircraft. A sort of welcome
gift.

Mountbatten   Excellent idea.

Eden   Very well. Bishop, could you make a note? We'll
inform the Ministry of Defence.

Macmillan   Although the Israelis may get unsettled if we're
seen to be arming Jordan.

Eden   Yes, perhaps. I'll telegraph Dulles in the States. Get
him to move on the offer of a few military bits and pieces for
the Israelis. That should keep them happy.

Mountbatten   Well of course, if we're doing that, may as
well make sure Iraq receives its tanks and equipment around
the same time.

Macmillan   Ah, then what about the Lebanese?

Eden   The Lebanese?

Mountbatten   Yes, they'll need something if we're giving
out to Israel.

Macmillan   And maybe the Sudanese.

Eden   Oh, for heaven's . . . fine, we'll just hand over HMS
Belfast!

Bishop (*writing*)   HMS –

Eden / Macmillan / Mountbatten (*together*)   No!

Eden   I think that should be enough for now, gentlemen.

Mountbatten (*pause*)   Hear the Americans pulled out of the Egyptian Dam deal.

Eden   Yes, which means we've pulled our support as well, I'm afraid. Though the danger is the Russians may get in there with funding now.

Mountbatten   Well, if you ask me it serves them right. Nasser blasting us on Radio Cairo. Ungrateful Arabs. If . . . ha! . . . if they don't give a dam, why should *we* give a dam! (*Laughs.*) Hope the Nile floods every day this year. (*Pause.*) Do you ever miss Durham, Prime Minister? Beautiful place. Wonderful cathedral, of course.

Eden   Oh yes. Stunning. I think one must always pine for one's first home occasionally.

Mountbatten   You know, I've always thought of Britain's geography like the anatomy of a woman. The top part is pretty enough, but can give you an awful lot of grief. When really, all the main action is from the Midlands down.

Eden (*pause. Mortified*)   Yes, that's . . . I've never thought of it in, uh . . .

Macmillan   Midlands down. Right.

Mountbatten   Though I always enjoy a good feel around the Pennines, what? (*Nudges* **Macmillan** *and laughs.*) Well now, I won't keep you, Prime Minister. Have to head off and pay a little visit to our base in the Falklands. Check everything's shipshape.

Eden   Yes, well. Thank you for stopping – Falklands! That's it! Falk –

He laughs, smiling smugly at **Bishop** *as he takes out the pad of paper and writes.*

Eden   Ha! Forty. There. Got them. (*Noticing his bemused company.*) Excuse me. (*Exits.*)

Macmillan   How is the mood in our forces, Dickie?

Mountbatten   Oh fine, Harold. Fine. Truth be told, as we shut up shop in more and more places, there's getting less and less for them to do!

Downing Street. **Eden** *is standing alone by a radio. The sound of an Arabic speaker exclaiming with passion. Suddenly, and slowly,* **Nasser** *appears some distance from him.* **Eden** *looks up, a mixture of fear and anger.* **Nasser** *smiles, then disappears.*

Prime Minister's chambers. Night. **Eden** *alone, as before. He looks panicked, mopping his brow and breathing heavily.* **Bishop** *bursts in, closely followed by* **Lloyd.**

Lloyd   Prime Minister. I've just heard.

Eden   Mr Lloyd. Mr Bishop. Sorry . . . uh, so sorry to drag you in so late.

Lloyd   Heavens, what . . . what on earth is that madman up to?

Macmillan *enters.*

Lloyd   Harold, Nasser has –

Macmillan   I know. The Egyptians have announced they're seizing control of the Suez Canal. (*Pause.*) I suppose we should have seen this on the cards.

Lloyd   Well, I didn't, and I'm Foreign Secretary! It's, it's . . . I mean, what is it?

Macmillan   It's intolerable.

Lloyd   You're right, in . . . intolerable! God, that man!

Eden   It's the seizing of international assets.

Lloyd   Seizing? It is tantamount to theft.

Macmillan   It is theft. (*Producing a note.*) Five million pounds withdrawn today from the Suez Canal Company account. From the Bank of Cairo.

Lloyd (*taking the note*)   That's our money!

Macmillan   So they're pickpockets as well. I can only assume it's a response to the United States and their withdrawal of aid towards their dam.

Lloyd   Well, that's not our fault!

Macmillan   We're all one. The West. It's an affront against us all.

Eden   And as such . . . as such, we respond, all of us, as one. The free world.

Macmillan   Prime Minister.

Eden (*beat*)   Dispatch telegrams to Paris and Washington immediately. I'll draft them.

Bishop   Prime Minister.

Bishop *exits.* **Macmillan, Lloyd** *and* **Eden** *look at each other. Pause.*

Eden   What . . . what does he think he's doing? This is just a, a, a blatant violation of international law, and a huge public slap in our face that we cannot tolerate. I will not . . . and the timing is incredible! We have King Feisal sleeping rooms away! It's been done to embarrass us. (*Pause.*) I MEAN, REALLY! Snatch and grab what isn't his. He, he's trying to humiliate us, damn it! (*He faces the Queen's portrait.*) How. Dare. He.

Macmillan   We must call the Cabinet to a meeting first thing tomorrow morning.

Eden   Then I must speak to the House.

Lloyd   I shall call the Chiefs of Staff to, um . . . God, to meet tomorrow as well.

Eden   Right.

Lloyd   I mean, no one is suggesting . . . You know, a response from our forces. It may not −

Macmillan   Although . . . quite. But. We must try and use this to our advantage.

Lloyd   Ad − ? What possible advantage can be − could be reaped from this?

Macmillan   Nasser is a ruthless dictator who has been troubling us for years. He's damaging our interests in the Middle East and threatening stability in the whole area. This is . . . well . . . an incentive to get the job finally done.

Eden (*pause*)   Overthrow his regime . . .

Macmillan   Whilst we're there . . .

Eden   You're right.

Lloyd   Prime Minister?

Eden   We've wanted him out for years.

Lloyd   But. If I, I could . . . you mustn't − we must wait to see what the situation is first.

Macmillan   The economic and trade situation is very dire indeed if Nasser obstructs our passage. He'll almost certainly use the revenue to fund the dam himself. More as an exercise in propaganda than because he actually cares for his people. Let alone what it would mean to our supply of oil!

Lloyd   Yes, but you're . . . I'm not disputing taking action on the Canal, against the breaking of UN regulations, but you're talking about deposing a / government.

Eden   No, but it's more than that! We've been here before, gentlemen. I've . . . I've been here before. When a dictator shows himself to have designs outside his nation and the world stands back until it's too late. Well. We stop this one dead before he gets going.

Macmillan   Agreed. We lose this one, we lose them all.

Eden   That man wants sole power in the Arab world, getting us out altogether. Leaving him free to suppress Jordan, Israel, the Sudan, whoever else he chooses.

Macmillan   Not to mention what signal this sends out to the world if a vicious dictator is seen to take what doesn't belong to him and then just get away with it.

Eden   Then we don't let him get away with it.

Lights down.

Act Two

Westminster. House of Commons. Loud commotion, which **Eden** *has to battle through.*

Eden No . . . no notice was given, no formal statement made. In truth, nothing that amounts to any kind of fair play. This is aggression. From an aggressive dictator. Of an aggressive regime. That has repercussions not just for our nation, but all nations, when the mutually agreed rules between countries are publicly disobeyed. Her Majesty's . . . Her Majesty's Government are acting swiftly in consulting the other governments of the world to assess this very serious situation, on a very international scale. May the House be assured that we will keep them informed!

War Rooms. **Mountbatten, Macmillan** *and* **Lloyd** *around a map on a table.* **Eden** *enters after* **Mountbatten** *has begun his analysis.*

Mountbatten Egypt. Its neighbours, Sudan and Libya. North-east we have Israel, Jordan, and here Saudi Arabia. Northern entrance to the Canal from the Med here. Southern exit to the Red Sea here. Port Said there. Alexandria here. Currently Port Said is the preferred choice of attack. Alexandria would be messier, with far more casualties.

Eden What are the Chiefs' suggestions on the kind of invasion force?

Mountbatten First assessments show that the most effective attack, certainly in terms of preparation time, would be paratroopers dropping here, at the northern entrance.

A phone rings. **Macmillan** *answers.*

Macmillan Macmillan.

Mountbatten Though it is incredibly perilous, as we know from our drops over Germany.

Eden   No. This is not to be a campaign that results in significant loss of life. On any side.

Macmillan   Thank you. (*Replaces the receiver.*)

Eden   We would lose all support.

Macmillan   That was the Minister for Fuel and Power. Our current oil reserves would last us six weeks, no more. Assuming the Egyptians place restrictions on our passage.

Lloyd   Good God, man!

Macmillan   Mr Jones and his staff are looking into the possibilities of sailing oil from the Persian Gulf around the Cape of Good Hope.

Lloyd   Oh crikey, they'd better set off now, then!

Eden (*to* **Mountbatten**)   What are the other initial suggestions?

Mountbatten   Well, there's the possibility of unilateral action from naval and marine forces. Send the Maltese fleet to Cyprus, pick up ten, twelve thousand marine commandos, sail them to Port Said. Could be there within four days, a touch more.

Lloyd   Though the problem then is maintaining control over the Canal once we are there.

Mountbatten   I agree. Troops on the ground, probably backed up by the RAF. (*Sighs.*) Truth be told . . . well, Britain does not really have the capacity for such an emergency.

Macmillan   We have the largest navy, one of the most feared armies and the most admired air force in the world. I'm pretty sure we do have the capacity.

Mountbatten   Yes, but this one is tricky. It warrants too small a campaign for a large-scale response. It's potentially very awkward. I mean the exact objectives are unclear.

Eden   The Cabinet objective is to place the Canal under a new international commission.

Mountbatten   Those are diplomatic objectives. What are our military objectives?

Macmillan   To seize the Canal by force if we have to.

Mountbatten   Well, with respect, I've never had to develop a strategy on such a basis.

Eden   Which is why we are pursuing all other possible alternatives. Political pressure backed up by the threat of military action. Only the threat.

Mountbatten   What's the situation regarding allied support?

Eden   From the French, definitely. They own shares in the company, and Nasser is involved in Algeria. This would be a war of revenge for them. And quite frankly, they're tired of being humiliated. This is a war they might actually win.

Mountbatten   And the Americans?

Eden   Eisenhower's reply to our telegram wasn't as outraged as I'd hoped. And there is the November election. Military support is unlikely, so we'll have to bank on moral.

The phone rings. **Lloyd** *answers.*

Lloyd   Lloyd.

Mountbatten   And, Mr Macmillan, not that I need to see a statement or anything, but . . .

Macmillan   Financial measures have been put in place. As for your budget, well, I'll need to sift around the piggy bank in more detail, but needless to say –

Lloyd   Thank you. (*Replaces receiver.*) Gentlemen. Our Cairo Embassy has been in touch.

Eden   Yes?

Lloyd   Our note of protest has been returned.

Eden   Returned? Any note?

Lloyd   Only . . . 'Return to sender'.

Eden (*pause*)   That devil.

Lloyd (*heading out*)   And I'm afraid Nasser has been making speeches again. One moment. (*Exits.*)

Eden   Well, that's it then. (*To* **Mountbatten**.) He's clearly not going to co-operate.

Lloyd *returns, holding a large file.*

Eden   That can't be all of it.

Lloyd   It's at least shorter than the last two-hour one. (*Reads.*) Shout. Scream. Uh, wave of fist. It is within his nation's right to nationalise what already belongs to them. Uh, and that the . . . imperial powers . . . have no case to claim any ownership themselves.

Eden   Imperial powers? (*Taking the transcript.*)

As the War Rooms darken, **Nasser** *appears in front of a microphone.*

Nasser   This, oh citizens, is the battle in which we are now involved. It is a battle against imperialism! In the past, they used to keep us waiting in the British High Commission! Now, they pay their dues to us! Arab nationalism has been set alight from the Atlantic to the Persian Gulf! Arab nationalism feels its existence and its strength!

Nasser *disappears as the War Rooms return.* **Eden** *overlapping slightly with* **Nasser**.

Eden (*reading*)   'This is not called the Suez Canal, it is called the Arabs' Canal' . . . 'The forces of Islam . . . ' (*Glancing up, somewhat fearful.*) 'are to clean the land . . . '

Macmillan (*pause. Turning to* **Mountbatten**)   A timetable of military operations as soon as possible, Lord Mountbatten.

Foreign Office. **Nutting** *enters to give* **Lloyd** *a report.*

Nutting   Our lawyers' findings.

Lloyd   Thank you, Nutting.

Nutting   It isn't promising, Foreign Secretary.

Lloyd   What do you mean?

Nutting   Based on the Joint Intelligence Committee report, Selwyn, and . . . and United Nations regulations, there is little to support a case for military action just yet.

Lloyd   What? Nasser has stolen international assets.

Nutting   He has nationalised a canal that runs through his land.

Lloyd   That isn't the point!

Nutting   I know, Selwyn. But no restrictions have been placed on our ships, even though they now pay their dues to Britain and not Egypt. He continues to employ all foreign nationals and the Egyptians, despite all fears, have proved capable of looking after the Canal themselves. Also, there has been . . . well, no real act of military aggression. If we launch a pre-emptive strike against a nation that hasn't fired one bullet, attacked one British citizen, Britain would be the aggressors. We who were the warmongers.

Lloyd *turns into the Prime Minister's chambers.* **Eden, Macmillan** *and* **Bishop**

Macmillan   I really don't see the problem, I'm afraid!

Lloyd   You don't see the problem / in this?! (*Waves the report.*)

Macmillan   We are responding to / an act of aggression.

Lloyd   The problem is we need an irrefutable legal case to show the world we are acting legitimately. Britain cannot just go to war whenever she feels like it! As it stands, I think, legally speaking, our position is very weak indeed.

Macmillan   Then we don't speak legally, we speak politically! Anthony?

Eden   We need to guard ourselves, yes, Selwyn.

Lloyd   Thank you.

Eden   But seeing as our standpoint legally is not the strongest it could be, I agree with Harold that we shouldn't . . . bring it up too often.

Macmillan   They're the ones who have acted illegally, Selwyn.

Lloyd   The Foreign Office cannot find substantial enough justification for war.

Macmillan   Then get them to try harder, damn it!

Lloyd   You want me to falsify intelligence!

Macmillan   We don't need to falsify intelligence! The world knows this is a vicious dictator. Their people will be grateful we overthrow him. As will the entire Middle East.

Lloyd   Why do you keep harping on about overthrowing him? One is one thing and one entirely another! I'm working on the basis of retrieving a canal. Through the right channels. Through the UN. Prime Minister, the Suez Canal Company is legally speaking a registered Egyptian Company operating under Egyptian law. He's compensating the shareholders. From a business point of view, he's . . . well, he's simply buying us out.

Eden   He's forcing us out.

Lloyd   It's his country.

Eden   It's our canal! We built it, we bought it, we own it.

Lloyd   I know, and I agree, both of you, Harold, you know I'm batting for the same team. But if we're accusing him of violating UN regulations, we can't respond by doing the same thing. Using these violations as an excuse to bring down a government we don't happen to like. This report bothers me. It bothers me, Prime Minister.

Eden (*pause*)   We will refer the matter to the UN Security Council.

Macmillan   Prime Minister, with all due respect, that would be / a waste of time.

Eden   Selwyn is right, Harold. We need to show the world we have every intention and every hope of sorting this out peacefully and diplomatically. And if that fails we then have no choice but to resort to the use of force. We need to push through a resolution.

Macmillan   They won't sanction any military action.

Lloyd   If we don't refer such matters to the UN then what is the point of this organisation? Why did we build it not even fifteen years ago? It means nothing.

Macmillan   Let us not forget this dictator has been flouting UN resolutions for years now, and the UN has done nothing. Which is precisely why we're going in to sort him out. Otherwise the UN really will mean nothing. That's the line we should take, Selwyn. That's what we should be focusing on, not the legality of a war, but the necessity for it. For international security against a mad dictator and his appalling regime! Winston would have razed Cairo to the ground by now, Anthony!

Eden   I understand, Harold.

Macmillan   And I am afraid I will have to resign if action is not taken. I cannot be a part of any administration that claims it will roar like a lion but hide like a mouse!

Eden   Harold –

Macmillan   And the Russians will only use their veto at the UN. They'll stop any resolution to take action against Egypt. You know they will, Anthony! So what is the point?!

Eden   MR MACMILLAN!

Macmillan (*pause*)   Prime Minister.

Eden   The point is to show the world that we tried. It clears our conscience. Which is also why I think we should accept America's request for a conference of the main maritime powers. As soon as possible. Mr Lloyd?

Lloyd   I'll get my staff onto it.

Eden   That will be all for now, gentlemen.

Macmillan *and* **Lloyd** *exit.* **Eden** *writes a note and hands it to* **Bishop**.

Eden   Fred, could you . . . my prescription for Evans. I want to up the dosage of Benzedrine, and uh . . . need more Sparine, and the, the purple ones. I can't remember their name.

Bishop   Prime Minister. (*Exits.*)

Downing Street. **Bishop** *and* **Clarissa**.

Clarissa   What do you mean?

Bishop   I am sorry, Lady Eden, but there's nothing all day. He can't fit you in.

Clarissa   He can't *what?*

Bishop   Uh . . .

Clarissa   Fit. Me. In?

Bishop   He has appointments. People have to book rather in advance at the moment.

Clarissa (*beat*)   Well, I'd better book an appointment, then.

Bishop (*pause*)   Beg pardon?

Clarissa   I would like to book an appointment with my husband, please.

Bishop (*beat*)   All right. (*Opens a diary.*)

Clarissa   Tomorrow morning?

Bishop   Sorry.

Clarissa   Afternoon? Evening?

Bishop   Nothing really all day, I'm afraid.

Clarissa   Night?

Bishop   I'm sorry?

Clarissa   Night.

Bishop   Well . . . you'll be . . . 'seeing' him . . . anyway. Won't you?

Clarissa   You would think so, wouldn't you?

Bishop (*writing*)   What business?

Clarissa *glowers at him.*

Bishop (*beat. Snapping the book closed*)   Right. There. You're in.

Downing Street. Prime Minister's chambers. **Eden** *and* **Macmillan**.

Eden   I received another telegram from Eisenhower. He's very worried we're too far ahead in our military plans. Thinks we've decided to go in guns blazing regardless of whether there's a diplomatic road to peace. He mentions you by name.

Macmillan   I'm touched.

Eden   Murphy relayed to him your talks. Sounds like you frightened the trousers off him.

Macmillan (*smiling*)   Really?

Eden   You're pleased?

Macmillan   The Americans will play along more readily if they think we're about to blow up the Middle East.

Eden   A rather dangerous game, Harold. Maybe play down the warlord rhetoric for now?

Macmillan   Very well. (*Beat.*) Prime Minister, I've reservations about the Port Said plan.

Eden   You . . . do?

Macmillan   I think it limits our outcome to regaining the Canal.

Eden   Which is our primary objective, Harold.

Macmillan   Publicly, yes. Though ultimately isn't it to overthrow Nasser?

Eden   You have a better one?

Macmillan   I think we should invade through Alexandria. That way we enter the Canal Zone from behind, get a foothold, and advance through the rest of Egypt.

Eden (*pause*)   Well. Run it past Mountbatten, if you'd like. Though, try to, uh . . . try to keep any paper trail to a limit, would you?

Macmillan   Prime Minister. (*Beat.*) And Prime Minister? Might it be time to involve Israel?

Eden   We've been in constant contact, of course. But perhaps it's not time to start enlisting other armed forces just yet, Harold. We need to show we're giving the conference and the UN a chance.

Macmillan   It's only that they are on the border, and what with all the militia attacks from Egypt, they have been desperate to overthrow Nasser for some time now. (*Pause.*) Just a thought, Prime Minister.

Downing Street. Prime Minister's chambers. **Eden** *and* **Nutting**.

Eden   Well, obviously the Foreign Office doesn't give a damn about British prestige, Mr Nutting, otherwise you wouldn't be doing all you could to hamper this campaign. If you got your way, Nasser will be the end of us! I mean, you, you've met him.

Nutting   Yes, Prime Minister, and I found him quite charming. A little brash / perhaps.

Eden (*laugh*)   Ch . . . charming? Ha!

Nutting   A full-scale invasion will only give Nasser more support amongst his Arab neighbours. I fail to see how that would neutralise him.

Eden (*pause*)   Neutralise him? Neu-tra-lise him? I want him gone. Do you understand? I. Want. Him. *Gone.*

Nutting (*pause. He nods, sadly*)   Prime Minister.

Downing Street. Bedroom. **Clarissa** *in bed,* **Eden** *getting ready to join.*

Clarissa   You're late.

Eden   Hmm?

Clarissa   For my appointment. I booked you in. And you look awful.

Eden   Thank you, darling.

Clarissa   And four a.m. is no time to be coming to bed. You'll be getting up in three hours.

Eden   Two. (*Taking his cycle of pills with a glass of water.*)

Clarissa   You should see Evans about getting off them. Apparently these amphetamines don't give you more energy, just use up what you have in bursts.

Eden   I need them at the moment, all right. The fevers and . . . pains have . . .

He clambers into bed and continues his cycle of pills.

Darling, you worked with this Anthony Nutting chap during the war, didn't you?

Clarissa   Yes, we decoded ciphers together in the Foreign Office.

Eden   What did you make of him?

Clarissa   I thought he was rather sweet. Why?

Eden   Hmm. Just . . . (*Sighs.*)

Clarissa   Anthony, the news said you lost your temper in the House today. Try to stay calm. It isn't professional. They're trying to provoke you, and you're letting them win.

Eden *turns off the light and the room descends into darkness.*

Westminster. Press room. **Reporter** *is note-taking,* **Caricaturist**
is sketching.

Reporter   See Egypt's rejected the conference demands.
And the UN aren't playing ball.

Caricaturist   So it would seem. (*Sucking in air through his
teeth.*) Looks like old Tony is taking the country to war, then.
Whether they like it or not.

Reporter   Judging from our poll this morning, they like it
not. Don't think a canal is worth a war. Think Egypt must do
something else first. Something worse.

Caricaturist   Reckon it'll harm our standing in the Middle
East, Bill. Make those Arabs hate us even more.

Reporter   Do they hate us, Fred?

Caricaturist   They distrust us.

Reporter (*sucking in air*)   Some tough decisions to be made at
the top then, eh?

Caricaturist Yup. Where do you stand?

Reporter   Where do I stand?

Caricaturist   Yes.

Reporter   I'd prefer to wait until the decision is proven right
or wrong, Fred. Then I'll choose to stand in the appropriate
place and say I have been standing there all along.

Caricaturist   Sounds like a good idea, Bill. Mind if I join
you?

Reporter   Not at all, Fred. There'll be plenty of room for
everyone.

Downing Street. Prime Minister's chambers. **Eden** *is on the phone,
writing notes. Newspapers cover his desk.*

Eden   Yes, well . . . (*Pause.*) But the four yellow ones at night
are, are the, um . . . the equivalent of two red ones, right?
(*Pause.*) Sometimes I find it better to take three yellows before

bed and then maybe a red one if I wake in the night. (*Pause.*) What green – I don't have any green ones. (*Pause.*) Well, can I get some green ones?

He writes some notes. **Bishop** *enters.*

Eden   OK. Yes. Bye. (*He writes, mumbling to himself.*) Red, green, blue, all the colours of the bloody rainbow. Right! Bishop.

Bishop   Lord Mountbatten and Mr Lloyd are here with the operation details, sir.

Eden   Have you seen these, Fred? (*Holding up the newspapers.*) Treacherous, the lot of them. Buckling under the pressure. Giving in to hysteria. Denouncing me one by one!

Bishop   That's not entirely the case, Prime Minister. Most bar a couple still support –

Eden   This one! Claims an increasing number of ministers are resigning! It's – how can any respectable government operate under such scrutiny? And betrayal!

Bishop   Right, well, we should get your press secretary to rush out a release stating these ministers aren't resigning over Suez.

Eden   I can't.

Bishop   Why not?

Eden   Because my press secretary has just resigned over Suez.

He swallows some tablets as **Lloyd**, **Macmillan** *and* **Mountbatten** *enter with plans.*

Mountbatten   Prime Minister.

Eden   Gentlemen. Let's get going on this, shall we?

Lloyd   I hear the French are getting impatient.

Macmillan   We're all getting impatient, Selwyn.

Eden   We mustn't dawdle. The people and the, the, the press have noticed we are arming ourselves but are seeing no action.

Mountbatten   How are they noticing?

Macmillan   Our navy has been on standby for a fortnight. And when you see tanks on the road painted a sandy colour you don't need to be Einstein to put two and two together.

Mountbatten   Christ! The secret service can't even fart any more without the press getting wind of it. (*Beat.*) So to speak.

Lloyd   Is everyone ready?

Mountbatten   Prime Minister, here is the joint plan of action as agreed by our Chiefs of Staff and the French officials. Alexandria will now be the landing point . . .

Eden *looks at* **Macmillan***, who doesn't flinch.*

Mountbatten   . . . the operation will consist of eighty thousand men, including one French regiment. Phase One will be the RAF bombing of Egyptian bases. Once the Egyptian air force has been annihilated, our troops hit the ground from the Med to take Alexandria.

Eden   The resistance in Alexandria was to be greater than in Port Said, I thought.

Lloyd   It will be easier to occupy the northern regions after Nasser is overthrown.

Eden   I wanted all options that prevented maximum casualties to be pursued. Is the speed of the Alexandria option really worth the extra loss?

Mountbatten   This is the joint recommendation from the French and ourselves. Our main problem then is our exit strategy.

Eden   What's the problem?

Mountbatten   We don't really have one. If we're successful in regaining the Canal and toppling Nasser, we would have to make the always awkward transition from invasion force to occupying force until a new administration can be placed in power.

Lloyd   Our prime concern would be to maintain good relationships with the locals. A Western army occupying an Arab country would do us few favours in the Middle East, let alone at home if we are there too long.

Eden   Well. Detailed plans for an exit strategy pending, I agree to sign these off. (*Taking the proposals.*) What is the code-name?

Lloyd   Ah. Now. I'm afraid 'Operation Hamilcar' can no longer work. Telegram from the French this morning. Apparently Hamilcar is, uh . . . well it's spelt differently in French.

Mountbatten   Differently?

Lloyd   It's spelt with an 'A', not an 'H', sir.

Macmillan (*sighs*)   Lord, all . . .

Lloyd   They want a different name. Make them feel more involved.

Eden   And what do they suggest?

Lloyd   Musketeer.

There is an eye-rolling from everyone.

Eden   Very French. Fine. (*Begins to write.*) Do they spell Musketeer the same way we do?

Lloyd   Uh, I assume so. Bishop?

Bishop   Yes they do, Prime Minister.

Eden (*starts to write. Pause*)   M-u-s?

Bishop   / M-u-s-k . . .

Macmillan (*overlapping*)   M-u-s-k-e-t.

Eden   E-t . . .

Macmillan   / Double 'e'.

Mountbatten   E-e . . .

Eden   Double E, e-e. That's four 'e's.

Macmillan   No, just –

Mountbatten   Just two 'e's.

Eden   Well can only one person speak, please?

They all start to spell it for him before **Macmillan** *breaks through as the loudest.*

Macmillan   M-u-s-k-e-t-e-e-r.

Eden   E-e-r. For heaven's sake, there . . . (*Thrusts the document in* **Mountbatten***'s hand.*) Right. Let's get this thing moving, shall we?

Television studio. **Eden** *sits in front of a camera, holding some notes. He shuffles in his seat, staring straight ahead. A stronger light shines on him, and he begins.*

Eden   Naturally no one wants a war. But sometimes the decision is not made by us. It is made for us. By those who disobey the rules. Those who threaten the security of their own people, and of the world. Yes, we could give him the benefit of the doubt. Just like we gave Mussolini the benefit of the doubt. Just like we gave Hitler the benefit of the doubt. But forgive me if I am no longer willing to take the word of such reckless, untrustworthy men and their regimes. And God forbid any nation that does.

Westminster. Press room.

Reporter   Taking his case direct into people's homes, Fred. That's a new one.

Caricaturist   Mm. Thought he came across rather well, Bill. For what good it'll do him.

Downing Street. Prime Minister's chambers. **Bishop** *with* **Eden**, *who slams down a pile of papers, knocking items off his desk.*

Eden   This is turning into a farce. A bloody farce! Can you believe it?

Bishop   It is unfortunate, Prime Minister.

Eden   Unfortunate?! It's like they're against me! First they want to change it to Alexandria. And now, now they're saying they've 'gone off' that and are back onto Port Said again. So. More time is needed. More time. Our armed forces will be in a state of readiness for the next seven years!

Macmillan *enters, holding up a document that he drops on the desk.*

Macmillan   Prime Minister. 'Musketeer Revise'.

Eden   Fred, could you . . . leave us, please.

Bishop *leaves.*

Eden   The Americans are worried about Russian intervention. Apparently they know of two Russian submarines that have taken on board Egyptian crews.

Macmillan   Naturally they're going to be . . . tetchy, Prime Minister. But when the campaign is completed successfully and Nasser overthrown, the Russians won't have an ally in Egypt. And the Americans will be thanking us.

Eden   Well, they needn't worry, anyway. Our generals take so long to get a war going, the Canal will have dried up before they finish! The French must be furious.

Macmillan   From what I hear, they're beginning to look elsewhere.

Eden (*sighs*)   The Israelis.

Macmillan   They're tired of waiting.

Eden   Well, do you know what . . . (*Trails.*)

Macmillan *fixes them a drink. He now talks in a very calm, dry and measured tone.*

Macmillan   I have been made aware, Prime Minister, that the French legal team are looking at the 1954 treaty on our troop withdrawals from the Canal. It states, signed by the Egyptians, that British troops can return in an emergency.

Eden (*pause*)   So I recall. But we've checked that. This doesn't constitute –

Macmillan   I know. It doesn't. But something else might.

Eden (*pause*)   I don't – what do you – ?

Macmillan   Oh I don't know. We're just talking. (*Pause.*) But so are the French and Israelis. They were just wondering what would happen if, say . . . the Israelis sent a ship down the canal.

Eden   The Israelis are sending a ship down the Canal?!

Macmillan   No, they're not. We're just talking. (*Pause.*) But what if they did?

Eden   The Egyptians would attack the ship, of course.

Macmillan   Yes, they would. There'd be a fight. There could be . . . a war.

Eden   Harold . . .

Macmillan   We're just talking, remember. Just talking.

Eden   We are?

Macmillan   Yes. We are.

Eden (*pause*)   If that happened, we would be under international obligation to –

Macmillan   – to intervene, and restore order –

Eden   – by occupying the Canal Zone –

Macmillan   – and placing it back under international control. Asking both sides to retreat a set distance away from the Canal. Say, ten miles. Including the Egyptians.

Eden   The Egyptians would never agree to that.

Macmillan   No, Anthony, you're right. They wouldn't.
Which means . . . regrettably, but legitimately . . . we would
have to use force against Nasser and his regime. Regrettably.
But. Legitimately. Prime Minister.

Eden (*pause*)   I, I've . . . fought against this kind . . . Fought
for peace my / entire –

Macmillan   You still are. We all are. You know what
appeasement of dictators means, Anthony. You more than
anyone.

Eden *looks at the portrait of the Queen.*

Eden   I remember the . . . the time I was at Stalin's war
rooms in Moscow. During the War. We were standing in front
of this huge map of the world. The size of a house. Discussing
various tactics and strategies. Stalin looked up at the map. At
Britain. Looked at me, and said, with a hint of awe and wonder
in his voice . . . 'How can so much depend on one tiny little
island?' And we both just stood there. Quietly. Looking . . .
(*Long pause.*) Send someone to Paris.

Macmillan   Prime Minister.

Eden   Discreetly.

Macmillan *smiles and toasts his glass.*

Macmillan   I've never been anything but, Prime Minister.

Downing Street. Back room. Dimly lit. **Eden** *and* **Lloyd**.

Eden (*holding a sheet of paper*)   There's written evidence!

Lloyd   There's –

Eden   Who gave you this?

Lloyd   It was drawn up at the Quai d'Orsay in Paris.

Eden   I cannot believe they have been so reckless! Why does
it need to be written down?

Lloyd   Something needs to be signed, Prime Minister.

Eden If this got out. If this got out do you realise . . . (*Begins to cough.*) . . . do you have any idea . . . (*Trails off into a coughing fit.*)

Lloyd There are only two, Anthony.

Eden (*regains himself*)   Burn this one.

Lloyd What?

Eden Burn it!

Lloyd *takes it.*

Eden And the other one?

Lloyd In a safe in the Quai d'Orsay. Signed by all of us, the French and Israelis.

Eden Send people over there. I want it destroyed.

Lloyd You . . . want it what?

Eden I WANT IT DESTROYED!

Lloyd W-what kind of people? Secret service?

Eden No! Not – this isn't espionage, for heaven's sake! Just anyone. Two chaps on your staff. Just get them over there and get that copy. I mean it. Now.

Lloyd Prime Minister.

Eden *disappears.* **Lloyd** *steps forward, and sets the document alight.*

Eden *reappears, sitting in the Prime Minister's chambers, head in his hands, looking devastated.* **Macmillan** *standing over him. Silence.*

Macmillan They did wait several hours in the foyer, Anthony. Before the French came out to say they would keep a copy intact. For their records. Although it's an irrelevance now. A third copy was made of the agreement for the Israelis in Tel Aviv.

Pause. **Eden** *doesn't move.*

Macmillan   No one will see it, Anthony.

Eden   In thirty years . . .

Macmillan   By then it won't make any difference.

Eden   My place in history . . .

Macmillan   There are more important things.

Eden   A canal?!

Macmillan   BRITAIN!

Long pause.

Eden (*looks up, determined*)   I know. (*Beat.*) It's just a shame, that's all. Just a shame.

Macmillan   We need to prepare. The Israelis are going in. The movement of troops to the Jordan–Israeli border is under way as a diversion. Make people think Israel have ambitions for Jordan not Egypt. (*Beat.*) Remember what Winston always said.

Eden (*sighs*)   What did Winston always say, Harold?

Macmillan   History is written by the winners. It will be written by us.

Nutting *bursts in, followed by* **Lloyd** *and* **Bishop**.

Bishop   Mr Nutting!

Lloyd   Anthony, stop!

Eden   What's happened?

Nutting   Prime Minister, please, I beg you. End this sordid conspiracy now, I beg you.

Macmillan   Mr Nutting! What is the / meaning of this?

Nutting   This is not only highly illegal but highly immoral and your motives are so transparent / the whole world will know your intentions!

Macmillan   Selwyn! Can you not keep your staff under control? This is obscene!

Eden It's all right, Harold, it's . . . it's OK. (*Pause.*) Nutting, I do understand –

Nutting Please. I beg, I beg you. It's not too late to seek a legitimate, peaceful route. This action is in breach of the UN Charter and of the Base Agreement which you and I constructed and signed not two years ago!

Eden Egypt broke that contract when they seized the Canal. They started this, man!

Nutting So this is how Britain conducts her affairs now? Tit for tat?

Macmillan Nutting! Don't forget whom you are talking to. Bishop?

Bishop Prime Minister?

Eden How dare you question my integrity!

Nutting Integrity?! (*Referring to* **Lloyd**.) I've had to watch my minister over the past week taking secret night flights to France. Shredding documents, burning files.

Eden We have nothing to hide!

Nutting Then why did you insist Bishop stop taking notes at the meeting with the French!

Eden How dare you! Do you know what, what I've, I've – how hard I have worked, how I have – my whole life dedicated to peace and, and . . .

Nutting I know of your impeccable record, Mr Eden, / that's why this shocks me so.

Eden Question my motives! I bloody well resigned from government over the appeasement of Hitler and, and the others! The lives, Nutting, the lives! That, that, that could have been saved! Well I won't / make the same mistake again!

Nutting Why have you got it into your head that Nasser is Hitler, Prime Minister?!

Eden   Why are you so keen to protect him? Can't you see /
what he's doing?!

Nutting   You told me never to make it personal! Never. Why,
why can't we follow through the good work Selwyn is doing at
the UN?

Macmillan   Because it isn't working!

Nutting   And you're willing to sacrifice British soldiers on
not trying!!

Macmillan   Get out, man! Bishop!

Bishop   Prime Minister?

Nutting   I am afraid I will have to tender my resignation,
Prime Minister.

Lloyd   Nutting, Israel is attacking Egypt tonight.

Nutting   Oh yes. Their 'surprise' attack. And then the
French arrive tomorrow under the pretence of drawing up an
ultimatum to the Israelis and Egyptians to cease fighting. An
ultimatum I have been asked to draw up *now*. To save time
tomorrow. Well, I won't. I won't. It is with a heavy heart,
Prime Minister, that I must resign my post. I cannot serve an
administration that chooses war as its first resort, not its last.
The shame! I mean . . . look at . . . Can any of you even look
me straight in the eye. Any of you?

Nutting *looks around at his company, all of whom shift their gaze,
except* **Macmillan**, *whom he comes to last.* **Eden** *starts shifting
things nervously on his desk.*

Eden   Well, you . . . I would have thought you'd have been
more concerned with, with the threat Israel poses to, to
Jordan, wanting to protect them.

Nutting   Oh yes, that's right. Though of course the Israeli
threat to Jordan was something we made up to distract the
international community. Wasn't it? Prime Minister?

Silence. **Eden** *looks down, shuffling papers with no purpose.*

Nutting   Already you're struggling to remember what is real and what is your fictional world of lies and deceit. (*Pause.*) You know what you look like to me, Prime Minister?

Macmillan   That's enough. Selwyn?

Lloyd   Come on, Nutting. Let's go. This is / no way to conduct –

Nutting   You look like a man who has seen his own terrifying downfall in front of him. I can see it in your eyes. The cavernous hole . . . getting bigger and deeper, spreading outwards, to swallow you up . . .

Eden, *eyes locked, begins to tremble.*

Eden   G-go . . .

Nutting   I tried, I did try!

Bishop   Mr Nutting, I must ask you to leave.

Nutting   But you won't even save yourself!

Macmillan   May I remind you you're talking to / the Prime Minister!

Eden   PLEASE STOP! GET HIM OUT!

Lloyd   Mr Nutting, please. / Prime Minister, I'm so sorry.

Eden   GET HIM OUT OF HERE!

Bishop *and* **Macmillan** *bundle him out.* **Lloyd** *follows.* **Eden** *collapses in his chair.*

Downing Street. Corridors. **Macmillan** *and* **Nutting**, *who holds a letter.*

Nutting   My resignation letter to the Commons. I have not included the details. For Anthony, you understand. Though I have a good mind to drop a copy off at the American Embassy. Alert Eisenhower of your plan. Stop this before it's too late.

Macmillan   No. You won't.

He takes the letter, and rips it in two.

For the good of the government, Mr Nutting. There's a good chap.

Macmillan *disappears.*

Clarissa *appears.*

Clarissa I don't suppose there's any chance you'll change your mind. For an old friend. For two.

Nutting I'm so sorry, Clarissa. It breaks my heart. But I can't betray it.

Clarissa (*getting upset*) He's going the wrong way, isn't he?

Nutting *pauses. Nods his head slowly.*

Clarissa I know it. I know it, I can . . .

Nutting Perhaps you could say something. They're all . . . we're of a, a different generation. You and I. We see the future when all they see is the past.

Clarissa Please don't judge him so . . . I see things you don't. There are things he . . . like . . . Don't tell him I spoke of this, but when he worked on the Anglo-Iranian oil deal as Foreign Secretary. Did you know he sold his shares in the company? To avoid a 'conflict of interest'. Despite it practically bankrupting him. He thought there were more important things than personal gain. I know you can't see that in him now but –

Nutting I can see that, now. That's why it . . . (*Pause. Sighs.*) That's *why*.

Clarissa You know, at the end of every day it feels as though he washes back to me like a tide. And every day it feels . . . like he washes out a little bit further. Each and every time. Until it feels like one day he won't come back at all.

Nutting I can't imagine how all this could ever be worth it. For you. How can it possibly be worth it?

Clarissa Because he's my husband. And when this is gone . . . I'm all he'll have. (*Pause. She laughs, tragically.*) He's already worried. About how he'll be remembered.

Nutting   Oh, Clarissa. I don't think you . . . quite understand.

Clarissa   Don't say that.

Nutting   He's going –

Clarissa   Don't ever say that to me!

Nutting   Forgive me. (*Pause.*) If it's any consolation . . . and I hope it is . . . I fear his premiership will be such an anomaly he will barely be remembered at all. (*Pause.*) I'm so sorry.

He disappears.

Downing Street. Prime Minister's chambers. **Eden** *enters looking exhausted. He closes the door behind him, and rests against it with his back. He is surprised to see the room is empty. He slams his briefcase onto the desk and storms back to the door.*

Eden   Hello?! Anyone there?!

He hops to the window and peeks out suspiciously. **Bishop** *enters.* **Eden** *spins.*

Eden   Where the devil were you?

Bishop   Prime Minister?

Eden   Everyone jumping ship now the going has got rough? Where were you?

Bishop   I'm not sure I understand, Prime Minister. I was . . . I was here.

Eden   You should have seen it, Fred. In the House. I announced our forces had set sail. There were nearly riots. They were actually . . . booing me. I thought I was going to have to, to leave for my own . . . (*Pause.*) Monckton's resigned from Defence, now. You heard that? It's all got so –

Macmillan *and* **Lloyd** *enter.*

Lloyd   Well, that was a sight.

Eden   Where have you been?

Macmillan   Anthony. (*Handing him a report.*) Transcript from the press conference in America. It's worse than we thought.

Eden (*taking it*)   Oh God . . .

Macmillan   Basically they've dissociated themselves from the whole situation. Eisenhower also . . . uh, implied . . . that they would never support a policy that is tantamount to . . . (*Sighs.*) an imperialist power trying hold together its empire.

Eden (*pause*)   What?

Lloyd   Correspondence in from others, I'm afraid, as well. New Zealand, India, Canada, all um . . . all denouncing our course of action and demanding we turn our vessels back.

Macmillan   And my conversation with Murphy in the States. They . . . well, rather resent the idea of us starting a war on the assumption they would join in. 'Like the last one'.

Beat. **Eden** *slams the document down.*

Eden   Like the last one?! This has got nothing to do with our empire! Or imperialism! Or . . . It is to do with right and to do with wrong! Not wanting to stick our flag everywhere!

The phone rings. **Bishop** *answers.*

Bishop   Bishop.

Eden   But, but that doesn't mean we'll just . . . sit back and allow it to be trampled on!

Bishop (*offering the phone to* **Lloyd**)   Mr Lloyd. The Foreign Office.

Macmillan   Last time I checked we were still a superpower that made its own decisions.

Eden   I have, I have Cabinet members resigning, a country divided, a parliament nearly in revolt. Our Commonwealth against us! And the press! Who still backs us in the press now, Bishop? What are they saying now?

Bishop   Um, I'm afraid there is some increasing anti-Tory sentiment over the handling of the crisis. Even in the *Telegraph*.

There is a gasp from all. **Lloyd** *puts the phone down.*

Lloyd   Right. That was the American Embassy. I think they smell a rat.

Macmillan   Why, what have they said?

Lloyd   The part of our ultimatum demanding both parties withdraw ten miles from the Canal. They say it reads like we drew it up long before Israel invaded Egypt.

Macmillan   They're bluffing, how could they possibly know we did that?

Lloyd   They . . . they just wondered, since our motive for sending in troops is to protect Egypt from Israel, and given that Egypt have managed to hold them at bay miles from the Canal, why we're moving Israel, the aggressors, *forward* sixty-five miles, and the victims we're defending . . . *back* one hundred and thirty-five.

Dumbfounded silence. Everyone turns to **Macmillan**.

Macmillan   Whoopsie.

Eden *sighs and rubs his head in disbelief. The phone rings again.* **Lloyd** *answers.*

Eden   We keep going. The fleet will be there any time now. Then we can sort this out.

Macmillan   We just need to remain calm and strong, Anthony.

Lloyd   OK. Right. Thank you. (*Replacing the receiver.*) Um . . .

Eden   What now?

Lloyd   Second query from the Americans. They wanted to know, if we're going in only to 'keep the peace', why flyers dropped from British planes have been retrieved, encouraging the people to . . . overthrow . . . Nasser.

Lloyd *winces. Everyone turns again to* **Macmillan**.

Macmillan   Whoo –

Eden   Whoopsie. Yes. Right. Can everyone leave me for a while.

Macmillan   Anthony –

Eden   I need to sort some things out on my own, Harold.

Lloyd   Perhaps a stirring speech in the Commons, Anthony. Bolster their patriotism. Think of Winston, think of all he would have –

Eden   WINSTON CHURCHILL IS NOT THE PRIME MINISTER! I AM!

Silence.

Eden   Who is?

Lloyd   You are.

Bishop   You are, sir.

Eden   Harold?

Macmillan   You are. Prime Minister.

Eden   Go. Now.

Westminster. Houses of Commons. Loud commotion. **Eden** *looks exhausted.*

Eden   There . . . there has been no collusion with Israel. We had . . . no . . . there was no foreknowledge of their attack. None. There was . . . *none.*

The commotion dies. **Eden** *is alone, looking incredibly sad. He takes some tablets.*

Downing Street. Noise of horns and a demonstration outside begins to grow. **Eden** *paces nervously.* **Macmillan** *stands calm and still.*

Eden   What's taking them so long?! How long ago did the fleet set sail?

Macmillan   They are on their way from Malta, Prime Minister. I realise it's frustrating, but it is a long way.

Eden   I know how far it is from Malta, Harold! Why wasn't this planned?

Macmillan   There is no deep-water port in Cyprus. The nearest / was Malta.

Eden   We should have deployed the fleet sooner. They were waiting –

Macmillan   Do you not think the world would have got rather suspicious if the peacekeepers had set sail *before* the war?

Long pause. **Eden** *looks indignant.*

Macmillan   The RAF is persisting in the bombing until the fleet arrive.

Eden   They're fast running out of targets.

Macmillan   With all due respect, Anthony, it was the emphasis you placed on sparing innocents that prompted the first phase of carpet-bombing / on military targets.

Eden   Whereas you would have just sent in the troops and performed a massacre!

Macmillan   I would have done what had to / be done, Prime Minister.

Eden   Excuse me for not wanting slaughter and torture and death.

Macmillan   Are you suggesting that –

Eden   I have lost a son in war, Harold. I do know what it is to fight and to, to sacrifice.

Macmillan   Anthony, I wasn't / suggesting for a moment –

Eden   Please remember that! I have fought. And I have seen what horrors –

Macmillan   Oh, and what was the Somme, Anthony?

Eden (*pause*)   Harold –

Macmillan   A shattered pelvis and months trapped in a hospital bed hasn't made me unsympathetic to the suffering of soldiers. And I resent the implication.

Eden (*pause*)   I . . . (*Sighs.*)

Macmillan   I know . . . when Simon . . . How hard –

Eden   The Cabinet will be reconvening. Though how we're supposed to think properly when we have that racket going on outside? Biggest peacetime rally ever, Harold. Something else for the history books!

Bishop *enters.*

Bishop   Prime Minister –

Eden   Not now, Fred, the Cabinet are returning to –

Bishop   My apologies, Prime Minister. But this urgent telegram from the Foreign Office. It appears . . . it appears the UN has called for a ceasefire between Israel and Egypt.

Macmillan   . . . I beg your pardon?

Bishop   And Egypt have agreed.

Eden   Oh heavens, no . . . (*Taking the note in dismay.*)

Bishop   The UN want to send their own peacekeeping corps in to occupy the area.

Eden   Before we've even got there . . . (*Pause.*) Leave us.

Bishop *leaves.*

Macmillan   Damn. We must inform the Cabinet at once.

Eden   We can't abort.

Macmillan   Prime Minister?

Eden   Well can we?

Macmillan   If there is a ceasefire between Israel and Egypt then what do we say as our reason for going in?

Eden   I don't know, but, but . . . if the UN are occupying the area, we lose all hope of seizing back the Canal, let alone toppling Nasser.

Macmillan   We need to think very carefully about what we are saying, Anthony. This is uncharted territory.

Eden   Yes, well, so is Egypt, but we're going in there! How close are they?

Macmillan   Couple of days.

Eden   Too close not to be pulled back?

Macmillan   Not in the eyes of the world. You are –

Eden   – never too close to war that you can't pull back. Yes, I thought so. (*Pause.*) We should stay on our course. And we'll have to . . . to veto the UN resolution to send in a peacekeeping force.

Macmillan   That would confirm everyone's suspicion we were in on this from the start.

Eden   What choice do we have? You, you . . . realise what it would mean? For me. If we pull back now. You realise what I would . . . have to do . . . (*Trembling and opening his pills.*)

Macmillan   Anthony?

Clarissa *enters.*

Clarissa   Harold, would you excuse us?

Macmillan   Lady Eden, we have to return to –

Clarissa (*gesturing to the pills*)   Is that dinner today?

Eden (*pause*)   Harold. I'll . . . be there in a, a moment.

Macmillan   Prime Minister, we –

Eden   Just one bloody moment, Harold.

Pause. **Macmillan** *exits.*

Clarissa (*her hand out*)   Give them to me.

Eden   I need them. They're keeping me alive . . .

Clarissa   You need to rest. You need to throw them away. We need to get away!

Eden   How can I do that?!

Clarissa   YOU'RE KILLING YOURSELF! (*Pause.*) If it's a choice between losing you or losing that bloody canal . . .

Eden   It would be more than just . . . (*Pause.*) I'm . . . sorry. I'm truly . . . if this doesn't . . . work out. I'm sorry for the things you're going to find out that I've done.

Clarissa   You could never do wrong by me. (*Pause. Softly.*) Let's just go.

Eden   What?

Clarissa   Let's just run away. Whilst no one's looking. We could climb up the vines on the back wall. Up onto the poplars. And over. Two fugitives. No one would ever know.

Eden *smiles faintly, though he begins to look as frightened as a child.*

Clarissa (*moving to embrace him, whispering in his ear*)   Leave all this behind. Dressed all in black. Run onto the Mall. Flag down a bicycle. I could distract them, and you push them off. I'll sit on the back and you could ride us through Trafalgar Square, all the way to the Embankment. We'll hire a boat. Sail down the Thames, take us all the way to the coast. Find a ferry that will take us to France. Then get a car, all the way down to the south coast. And live out our days, together, in the sun . . .

Eden *smiles weakly, leaning against* **Clarissa**, *as they rock, back and forth, slowly . . .*

Clarissa   Remember when we used to dance . . .

In the distance, muted, a shell goes off. Then another. Louder. There is machine-gun fire. And tanks. And planes swooping over. Lights fade on **Clarissa** *and* **Eden**.

Westminster. Press room.

Reporter   Would you have it?! Nasser's gone and sunk his own ships, blocking the Canal!

Caricaturist   Sneaky, Egyptians. Always said it. Sneaky. (*Beat.*) Bloody good idea, though.

Reporter   Oh yeah. Smashing. (*Pause.*) Makes you wonder. How it's all going to end.

Downing Street. Prime Minister's chambers. **Eden** *and* **Bishop**.

Eden   Always, always rely on, on the opposition party to change with the tide. One minute they're this, the next they're that! And what are these whispers about Mountbatten? Hmm, Fred? What's he been saying?

Bishop   Uh, he . . . that he was never completely convinced by the operation.

Eden   Well, this is the first I've heard of it!!

Bishop   Apparently he talked his opinion through with a few Cabinet members.

Eden   Oh well that's fine then. As long as my Chief of Staff mentioned his opposition to the war he was running to *some ministers*, that's absolutely bloody fine. Any news?!

Bishop   None since this morning, Prime Minister. Our troops are still holding on to Port Said, though there has been more bloodshed and resistance than expected. And . . . messages are still coming in from a rather . . . disgruntled international community.

Eden *raises his hands in frustration.* **Macmillan** *and* **Lloyd** *burst in. Pause.*

Macmillan   Imagine what is the worst thing that could happen to us?

Eden (*pause*)   The last time I heard that, the King was dead. (*Sighs, and laughs as though he no longer cares.*) What? What's the next 'worst' thing that could happen?

Macmillan   The Russians have announced their alliance with Egypt against us.

Blood drains from the frozen **Eden***'s face. He smiles and shakes his head.*

Eden   Well I guess. That. Makes. Sense. (*Long pause.*) How, um . . . how confirmed?

Macmillan   Unconfirmed from Moscow. No formal declaration of war. But they are moving troops, Anthony . . .

Eden   Weapons?

Lloyd   Uh, I could . . . I could get the Foreign Office to . . .

Eden   Atomic weapons?

Lloyd   Probably . . .

There is a deathly silence. **Eden** *covers his mouth with his shaking hand.*

Lloyd (*attempting a joking tone*)   Although . . . if it's any consolation, not as many as us.

Eden (*whispering*)   Oh God. We've . . . (*Laughs, tragically.*) I've started World War Three.

Macmillan   We may have to consider moving you out of London, Anthony. Just in case.

Eden (*whispering*)   Oh God . . .

Macmillan   And, um . . . as expected, the Americans are . . . well . . . they're furious. Anthony. War with Russia is exactly what they feared would happen.

Lloyd   I contacted Dulles immediately. Asked them not to say anything / in public.

Macmillan   They are demanding we withdraw our forces immediately or else.

Eden (*looking up in horror*)   Well, since . . . since when do they . . . we, we . . . (*Looks to the others for show of confidence.*) We have a job to do. Right?

Lloyd   We asked for a guarantee that they would not, um . . . that they would not fire upon any British ships entering the Persian Gulf. They said . . . (*Deep breath, trying to steady his nerves.*) They said they couldn't necessarily give us that guarantee.

Eden   They . . . they'd shoot at *us*. The Ameri . . . the Ameri . . . (*Begins a coughing fit that he slowly gets under control.*) Why . . . why did it take us so long? I thought . . . our navy . . .

Macmillan   It's just one of those things, Prime Minister.

Eden *slams his fist down onto the desk several times in succession. The others take a step back.* **Eden** *stops and holds his hand to his mouth to stop any more coughs. As he speaks, he begins to shake, and it gets worse as he goes on.*

Eden   How did . . . we used . . . we used to be . . . used to have – and now . . . what? We're . . . wrists slapped and being told . . . what? To, to . . . it's, it's our canal. If we . . . if we . . . if we . . . a canal . . . If we can't even . . . even . . . A CANAL! (*Quieter.*) Canada. Australia . . .

Bishop   Prime Minister?

Eden   Falklands, Australia, Hong Kong, Singapore, Kenya. Yes, Kenya, must . . . mustn't . . .

Bishop   Anthony?

Eden (*steadying himself. Pause*)   Go.

Lloyd   Anthony, please.

Eden   Leave me. Please. I just need . . . go . . .

The others exit. **Eden** *takes a deep breath and tries to take a few steps forward. He starts to shiver violently, and bends over double.*

The map of the world grows brighter as Downing Street disappears. **Eden** *looks up, as the tango theme begins and* **Dulles** *appears.* **Eden** *makes to get into the dancing position, but* **Dulles** *spins on his heel, and holds* **Nasser**, *who appears behind him.*

Eden *watches aghast as they dance.* **Schuman** *appears and, ignoring* **Eden**, *cuts in on* **Dulles** *and* **Nasser** *as they interchange in the dance.* **Eden**, *hyperventilating, goes to grab* **Nasser** *by the neck, as* **Schuman**, **Dulles** *and* **Nasser** *disappear. Downing Street returns.* **Eden** *collapses back against his desk, exhausted and afraid.*

Macmillan *appears. Standing in front of a closed door. A* **Minister** *comes out.*

Minister   You can go in. Don't say anything to upset or worry him. He is still very weak.

The **Minister** *exits.* **Macmillan** *walks through the door. A light shines from one side, out of our view. He turns to face it, and smiles.*

Macmillan   Hello Winston. (*Pause.*) Got a minute?

Downing Street. Prime Minister's chambers. **Eden** *enters with* **Clarissa**'s *help. He rests on the edge of the desk, as* **Bishop** *follows with* **Lloyd** *and* **Macmillan**.

Bishop   Glad to see you're feeling better, Prime Minister.

Lloyd   Absolutely. Damn glad, Prime Minister.

Macmillan   Very glad, Anthony.

Eden (*almost inaudibly*)   What . . . ? (*Clears his throat.*) What news?

Lloyd   The, uh . . . the tangible gains we made before the ceasefire are looking untenable with the resistance plus the Russian threats. The United Nations welcome our willingness to the discussion of a United Nations force.

Macmillan   The Chiefs of Staff have drawn up three possible courses of action. One: to renew military action and occupy the whole canal. Two: maintain our position until a UN force is ready to take over. Or three . . . a complete withdrawal.

Lloyd   But the Americans will not allow a UN force to assume control until the Anglo-French contingent has withdrawn and . . . well, buggered off home, Prime Minister.

Macmillan   And I'm afraid the United States refuse to, uh . . . prop up our sterling until we're out completely, Prime Minister.

Eden *wraps himself up warmer. There is complete silence.*

Eden   Withdraw . . .

Lloyd (*unable to hear*)   I'm . . . sorry?

Eden (*louder*)   Withdraw . . .

Lloyd   Yes, Prime Minister.

They all exit. **Eden** *stands weakly, and totters around, without purpose. He looks at the Queen's portrait. The figure of* **Churchill** *slowly appears behind him.* **Eden** *turns to face him. Both look weak and feeble relics. Elgar's 'Nimrod' creeps softly in.*

Eden   Who could ever follow you?

Churchill   'For what shall it profit a man if he shall gain the whole world . . . and lose his soul?'

Eden   I . . . f-failed . . .

Churchill   This was just our time, Anthony. Just our time.

Eden   You were the saviour of Britain. And I . . . I am her undertaker.

Churchill (*shakes his head*)   Undertakers are not responsible for the deceased, Anthony. They merely see them safely down.

Eden   . . . After me?

Churchill   Macmillan . . .

Eden (*pause*)   I sh-should have been . . . stronger . . .

Churchill   You can deny, and ignore, the diminishing strength of something, and convince yourself, despite its age, it is as strong as those younger and healthier than he. But the time will always come . . . when you must decide . . . to sit this one out . . .

He moves to **Eden**, *and pulls him into him, as the music swells and lights fade.*

Churchill   My Anthony . . .

Eden *and* **Clarissa**'s *garden.* **Eden** *is sitting in a chair, covered in blankets, eyes closed and breathing heavily.* **Clarissa** *enters, followed by* **Bishop**.

Clarissa   Anthony? (*Pause.*) Anthony, look who's here.

Eden (*slowly opening his eyes, weakly*)   F-fred?

Bishop   Anthony. No, please don't get up.

Eden (*smiling*)   Fred. What a wonderful surprise. What are you doing here?

Bishop   Well I was passing and couldn't very well not pop in to see my old boss, could I?

Eden   Fred, it's wonderful to see you. How are things? How's . . . Harold?

Clarissa   Anthony.

Eden   I'm only asking.

Bishop   So-so. He's run into a few problems with his 'Never had it so good' claim.

Eden   Oh dear, too bad. (*Beat. Smiles.*) You must . . . Clarissa, we must show Fred our cow in the field. Fine heifer. We entered her into the local fair. And look, have you seen our bluebells?

Bishop   Yes, they're lovely. (*Beat. Laughs.*)

Eden   What?

Bishop   I'm in the Garden of Eden.

Clarissa   Let me fetch you a glass of lemonade, Fred. (*Exits.*)

Bishop   Lovely. Thank you.

Eden   It's wonderful. You know. Fred. Gardening. Just wonderful . . . Plant a seed, watch it grow. Tend to it. Care for it. Simple, and . . . and honest. (*Long pause.*) To wait so long, Fred . . . only to become the shortest serving Prime Minister of this century. And the shortest bar just three in nearly one hundred and fifty years.

Bishop   You're *not* the shortest?

Eden   Alas. Rosebery and Canning, last century. And Bonar Law in '22, in for just two hundred and nine days. Died of throat cancer.

Bishop   Oh. That's a relief then. (*Pause.*) As one last task, I could always compile an official report? (*In knowing jest.*) See how badly you really do compare?

Eden   I'm all right, actually, Fred.

Butler   Very good, Prime Min . . . Anthony.

Pause. They smile. **Clarissa** *enters with a glass of lemonade.*

Eden   Win . . . Winston's funeral, Fred . . . the whole nation. Mourning. Did you see? All the cranes in London, bowing their head . . . as his coffin sailed across the Thames. The whole city, the whole country . . . leaning with them . . . onto their knees.

Eden *closes his eyes, and rests his head back.* **Bishop** *places his hand on his.*

Clarissa   Fred, dear. Would you mind running into the kitchen? His tablets are on the side.

Bishop   Uh, yes. Yes, of . . . of course.

He exits. **Clarissa** *gets to her knees, by* **Eden.** *He looks at her.*

Eden   I know they will never bow for me. They loved him so much . . .

Clarissa   Come on. Stand up. It's getting cold.

She helps him to his feet. Pause.

Eden   After him, they had no more left to give. That love . . .

Clarissa   It isn't real, Anthony. This . . . this is real. And it's all that matters in the world . . .

The waltz theme creeps in. The map of the world beneath them twinkles again. **Eden** *and* **Clarissa** *embrace, and begin slowly to turn and move across the world together.*

Methuen Drama Modern Plays

include work by

Edward Albee
Jean Anouilh
John Arden
Margaretta D'Arcy
Peter Barnes
Sebastian Barry
Brendan Behan
Dermot Bolger
Edward Bond
Bertolt Brecht
Howard Brenton
Anthony Burgess
Simon Burke
Jim Cartwright
Caryl Churchill
Complicite
Noël Coward
Lucinda Coxon
Sarah Daniels
Nick Darke
Nick Dear
Shelagh Delaney
David Edgar
David Eldridge
Dario Fo
Michael Frayn
John Godber
Paul Godfrey
David Greig
John Guare
Peter Handke
David Harrower
Jonathan Harvey
Iain Heggie
Declan Hughes
Terry Johnson
Sarah Kane
Charlotte Keatley
Barrie Keeffe

Howard Korder
Robert Lepage
Doug Lucie
Martin McDonagh
John McGrath
Terrence McNally
David Mamet
Patrick Marber
Arthur Miller
Mtwa, Ngema & Simon
Tom Murphy
Phyllis Nagy
Peter Nichols
Sean O'Brien
Joseph O'Connor
Joe Orton
Louise Page
Joe Penhall
Luigi Pirandello
Stephen Poliakoff
Franca Rame
Mark Ravenhill
Philip Ridley
Reginald Rose
Willy Russell
Jean-Paul Sartre
Sam Shepard
Wole Soyinka
Simon Stephens
Shelagh Stephenson
Peter Straughan
C. P. Taylor
Theatre Workshop
Sue Townsend
Judy Upton
Timberlake Wertenbaker
Roy Williams
Snoo Wilson
Victoria Wood

Methuen Film titles include

The Wings of the Dove
Hossein Armini

Mrs Brown
Jeremy Brock

Persuasion
Nick Dear after Jane Austen

The Gambler
Nick Dear after Dostoyevski

Beautiful Thing
Jonathan Harven

Little Voice
Mark Herman

The Long Good Friday
Barrie Keeffe

State and main
David Mamet

The Crucible
Arthur Miller

The English Patient
Anthony Minghella

The Talented Mr Ripley
Anthony Minghella

Twelfth Night
Trevor Nunn after Shakespeare

The Krays
Philip Ridley

The Reflecting Skin & The Passion of Darkly Noon
Philip Ridley

Trojan Eddie
Billy Roche

Sling Blade
Billy Bob Thornton

The Acid House
Irvine Welsh

Methuen Drama Contemporary Dramatists
include

John Arden (two volumes)
Arden & D'Arcy
Peter Barnes (three volumes)
Sebastian Barry
Dermot Bolger
Edward Bond (eight volumes)
Howard Brenton
  (two volumes)
Richard Cameron
Jim Cartwright
Caryl Churchill (two volumes)
Sarah Daniels (two volumes)
Nick Darke
David Edgar (three volumes)
David Eldridge
Ben Elton
Dario Fo (two volumes)
Michael Frayn (three volumes)
David Greig
John Godber (four volumes)
Paul Godfrey
John Guare
Lee Hall (two volumes)
Peter Handke
Jonathan Harvey
  (two volumes)
Declan Hughes
Terry Johnson (three volumes)
Sarah Kane
Barrie Keeffe
Bernard-Marie Koltès
  (two volumes)
Franz Xaver Kroetz
David Lan
Bryony Lavery
Deborah Levy
Doug Lucie

David Mamet (four volumes)
Martin McDonagh
Duncan McLean
Anthony Minghella
  (two volumes)
Tom Murphy (six volumes)
Phyllis Nagy
Anthony Neilsen (two volumes)
Philip Osment
Gary Owen
Louise Page
Stewart Parker (two volumes)
Joe Penhall (two volumes)
Stephen Poliakoff
  (three volumes)
David Rabe (two volumes)
Mark Ravenhill (two volumes)
Christina Reid
Philip Ridley
Willy Russell
Eric-Emmanuel Schmitt
Ntozake Shange
Sam Shepard (two volumes)
Wole Soyinka (two volumes)
Simon Stephens (two volumes)
Shelagh Stephenson
David Storey (three volumes)
Sue Townsend
Judy Upton
Michel Vinaver
  (two volumes)
Arnold Wesker (two volumes)
Michael Wilcox
Roy Williams (three volumes)
Snoo Wilson (two volumes)
David Wood (two volumes)
Victoria Wood

Methuen Drama World Classics

include

Jean Anouilh (two volumes)
Brendan Behan
Aphra Behn
Bertolt Brecht (eight volumes)
Büchner
Bulgakov
Calderón
Čapek
Anton Chekhov
Noël Coward (eight volumes)
Feydeau (two volumes)
Eduardo De Filippo
Max Frisch
John Galsworthy
Gogol
Gorky (two volumes)
Harley Granville Barker
　(two volumes)
Victor Hugo
Henrik Ibsen (six volumes)
Jarry

Lorca (three volumes)
Marivaux
Mustapha Matura
David Mercer (two volumes)
Arthur Miller (six volumes)
Molière
Musset
Peter Nichols (two volumes)
Joe Orton
A. W. Pinero
Luigi Pirandello
Terence Rattigan
　(two volumes)
W. Somerset Maugham
　(two volumes)
August Strindberg
　(three volumes)
J. M. Synge
Ramón del Valle-Inclán
Frank Wedekind
Oscar Wilde